I0540206

DREAMS OF
A VILLAGE BOY

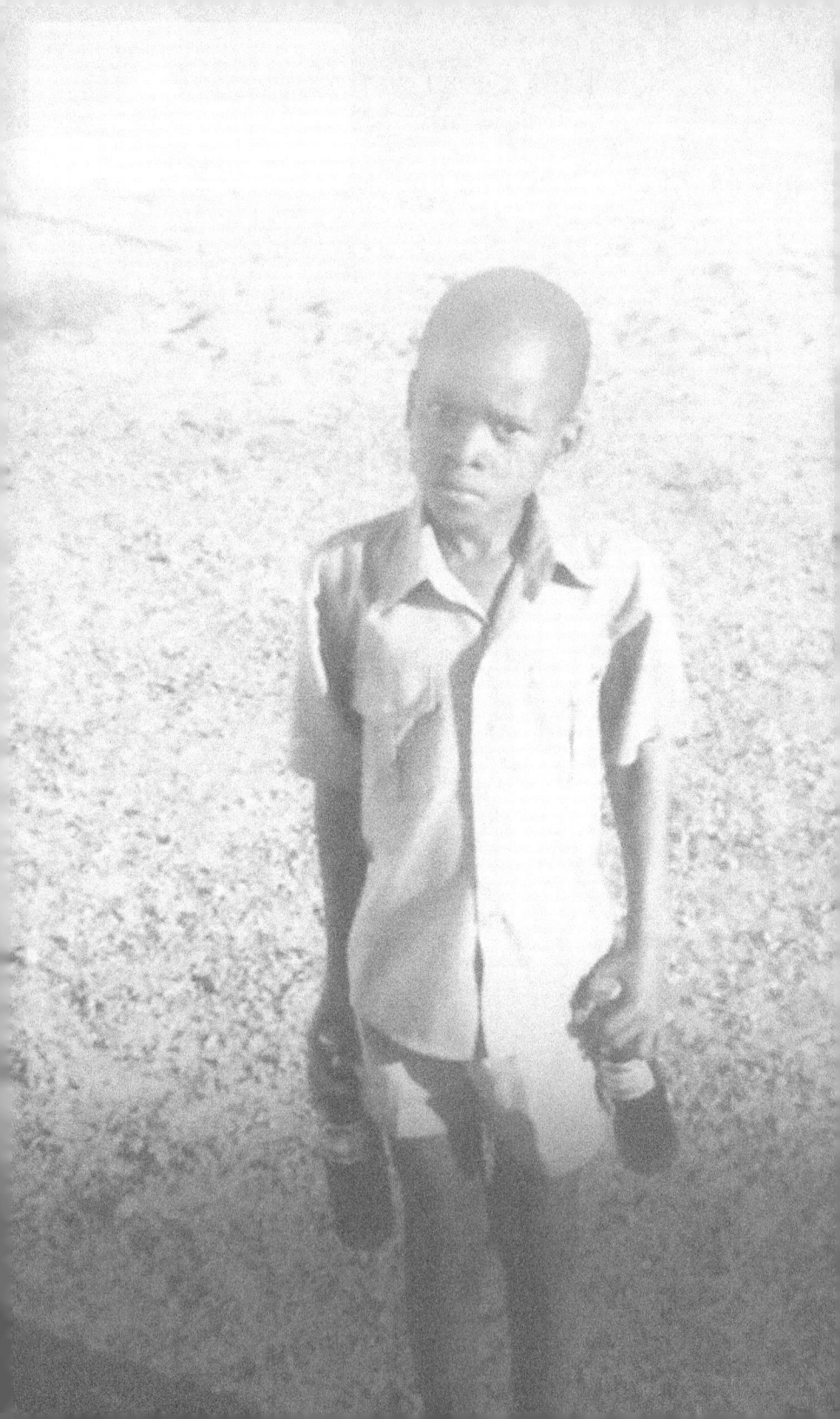

DREAMS OF A VILLAGE BOY

My Journey
From **AFRICA**
to **AMERICA**

ASHLEY R. SHUMBA

DREAMS OF A VILLAGE BOY
My Journey From Africa to America

Copyright © 2025 by Ashley R. Shumba

All rights reserved. No part of this book may be reproduced, distributed, or transmitted in any form or by any means, including photocopying, recording, or other electronic or mechanical methods, without the written permission from the publisher or author, except as permitted by U.S. copyright law or in the case of brief quotations embodied in a book review.

Disclaimer: Although the publisher and the author have made every effort to ensure that the information in this book was correct at press time and while this publication is designed to provide accurate information in regard to the subject matter covered, the publisher and the author assume no responsibility for errors, inaccuracies, omissions, or any other inconsistencies herein and hereby disclaim any liability to any party for any loss, damage, or disruption caused by errors or omissions, whether such errors or omissions result from negligence, accident, or any other cause.

Scriptures taken from the Holy Bible, New International Version®, NIV®. Copyright © 1973, 1978, 1984, 2011 by Biblica, Inc.™ Used by permission of Zondervan. All rights reserved worldwide. www.zondervan.com The "NIV" and "New International Version" are trademarks registered in the United States Patent and Trademark Office by Biblica, Inc.™

Interior Layout and Design by Stephanie Anderson
Book Cover Design by Abigael Elliott
Editorial Team: Mandi Reed, Cindy Venable

ISBNs:
979-8-89165-223-1 *Paperback*
979-8-89165-224-8 *Hardback*
979-8-89165-225-5 *E-book*

Published by:
Streamline Books
Kansas City, MO
streamlinebookspublishing.com

CONTENTS

DEDICATION

I wholeheartedly dedicate this book to my late father, Anania Shumba, who passed on in 2020 during the COVID-19 pandemic; my late uncle, Biriam Wabatagore, who died in a car accident in 2004; and my mentor Brian Dawkins, NFL Hall Of Fame.

My late father, Anania, who was a public schoolteacher, always used to say, "Education and moral values are the very core foundation of a society. Be grateful for the environment in which we have raised you—don't shame it but be proud of it. One day your village will be the foundation of your success. The poverty and struggle in this village is a sign of divine favor from God. Hunger breeds character and makes people creative and innovative. Great leaders come from humble environments. If you work hard, you can get ahead. Be someone our youngsters will one day look up to." Thank you, Daddy, I will forever make you proud. Continue to rest in peace!

My late uncle, Biriam, who was a very successful lawyer in Zimbabwe, guided me explicitly about the importance of the rule of law. When I became self-employed as a teenager, my uncle became my mentor. On the weekends, when we were at home relaxing, he used to impart to me words of wisdom like, "Ash, never be afraid to negotiate, and always be vigilant. Investment and business partnership must never be born of sympathy or favor. They are very practical processes that involve security, accountability, responsibility, transparency, and good values. Choose your friends wisely. Life's not a speed race, but a cross-country journey. Be patient and realistic about your dreams." Thank you, Uncle Biriam! The seed that you planted is growing and glowing. Rest in peace!

My mentor Brian Dawkins Sr. saw the best in me. Thank you so very much, my brother. Today, we are all reading this book about my life because of you. Although I have been offered help or guidance in the past, none matched the heights of your kindness. Because you took me under your wing, I rose beyond what I ever believed I could. You saw through ego to the potential beneath, and there is no greater gift you could have given me. You saw the best in me and decided to cowrite the book with me and boost my visibility to ensure many people get to hear about this unique, inspiring journey of mine. You are truly a godsent person. Honestly, how many celebrities or NFL Hall of Famers, who have met a random immigrant, took the time to listen to his story, put time and resources into getting his life story out into the world, and uplift his living standards? Many people admire our collaboration and speak so highly of your humility, remarkable character, and faith in God. I am blessed indeed to call you my prayer partner, mentor, brother, and friend. May the Lord continue to guide us through the many projects we have initiated for the benefit of the less privileged both in America and Africa. God bless you, my brother, and your wonderful wife and amazing children!

BLESSED FOREWORD

There was a time that I believed in coincidences, but I know better now.

My friend Ashley Shumba's story is one that could be written off as a collection of coincidental moments, but I believe it is a story of divine interventions and appointments. Why? Consider this: how often do you walk down the street and happen to see someone you can help? How often do you actually stop to help them? And how often does that person turn out to hold the exact key you need—one that will unlock the next door to your future blessing—and how often do they actually share that key with you?

In my experience, these kinds of things don't just happen—well, unless you're Ashley Shumba, that is. If you're him, they happen over and over and over again, in various countries and continents, and at various times throughout your life.

At this point you may be thinking, *Why Ashley? What makes him so special?*

The Bible exhorts us not to despise small beginnings, and Ashley's story perfectly demonstrates why this is wise counsel. As Ashley himself will tell you in the coming pages, he comes from a humble, meager environment that lacked the resources and infrastructure to provide many things for him and his family. Importantly, that did not stop him from reaching out of his comfort zone, time and time again, to help and be a blessing to someone else.

Neither did the many setbacks he experienced keep him from helping and striving, dreaming and hoping. None of those setbacks diminished his willingness to help or his ability to persevere. Ashley's particular perseverance, his stick-to-itiveness, his willingness to work and grind, and his determination to live in a spirit of expectant hope has allowed him to be in the space he occupies today.

To me, Ashley's attitude of perseverance and expectant hope demonstrates faith. I'm referring to Ashley's personal faith in God, of course, but also, on a larger scale, to what God says our faith in him should be.

I assure you that kind of faith takes courage—the same kind of courage Ashley demonstrated each time he had to encourage himself after a trial or setback.

Whether or not you believe you have courage inside of you, you did not come up with it on your own, and it has been placed there in seed form by the Lord. The phrase or commands *take courage, do not fear, be encouraged*, etc. appear in the Bible over 365 times. A good word of courage for every day of the year, and then some.

Every good and perfect gift comes from God. Consider Joshua, whom God commanded to be encouraged. "I am with you, I go before you," God said, "be encouraged." Remember, God will never command us to do something he has not equipped us to do, through faith in him.

When he commands us to "be encouraged," as he commanded Joshua, he is saying, "There is courage in you; let it come out."

And that is exactly what Ashley has done.

In addition to perseverance and faith, Ashley has also always had a gift of a vision, specifically to come to America. I've already spoken about his setbacks, but it's important to recognize that Ashley has also experienced great success. He has had plenty of opportunities to remain where he was and enjoy a comfortable, prosperous life. I, for one, am glad he chose differently, because faith does not grow in comfort. Comfort is like milk. It has an expiration date, and eventually it's gonna start stinkin'.

But to whom much is given, much is required. When we are given gifts, our job is to work to refine them unto the glorification of God and be a blessing to his people. Ashley is one of those individuals God has blessed with immense gifts and opportunities. Yes, he could have fallen in love with the place God put him at any given moment and stayed there, but that's not what God has called him (or any of us, for that matter) to do.

Ashley's vision told him there was more for him to do and more people for him to reach. I believe that vision—the one that pressed him to leave the village he was born in, and every other place in the world where he experienced growth and good success—was a vision from God. To me, that vision is made of similar stuff as what God was speaking about in Hosea 4:6: ". . . my people are destroyed for the lack of knowledge."

And Proverbs 29:18: "Where there is no revelation [vision from God], people cast off restraint [perish]; but blessed is the one who heeds wisdom's instruction."

It was, and remains, a vision that kept his son Ashley from perishing. And as Ashley's story—his testimony—so powerfully demonstrates, having a sense of what our tomorrow could possibly be, making that vision plain (as God told Habakkuk), and then trusting God to direct our steps (or our missteps) even when we are yet in a painful place, provides the strength we need to keep movin', to keep pushing through.

Ashley has the knowledge and understanding to do that—and when I say knowledge I'm referring to knowledge of living a life empowered by the Holy Spirit inside you. It's the ability to have a heavenly perspective on Earth. When we receive Jesus and are thus enlightened by the light of God, it's also the power we are given and walk around with each day. The word of God is undefeated. On the day Jesus returns, he will speak and again victory will be assured. His armies will not even have to fight because of the word of his mouth, his sword. (See Revelation 19:15.)

Our words too have power, and when we receive Jesus, they become the sword against the evil one and his agendas. On the day I met Ashley, a miscommunication led me to pray for guidance and patience so that my words conveyed God's grace instead of the human frustration I felt at the time. I was tired and did not feel like being there to play golf at the Eagles' autism event. I had given my word, though, so I showed up. Still, my attitude was not one that reflected Jesus, so I prayed quietly for a shift from me-focused to others-focused.

God was faithful. The wonderful, peace-filled change in my headspace that followed gave me the opportunity to ask what I often do when someone crosses my path and is driving me somewhere.

"Ashley," I said, "What is your big vision or dream?" As he related his life story to me, I consistently heard a positivity in him in the midst of uncomfortable and downright painful places. I could tell he was able to see things through a different, ever positive lens, and I could sense a real, abiding hope in him. Knowing that, I could not help but ask, "Do you see the hand of God moving you around and even bringing you to this moment, this conversation?"

I certainly saw it, and I still do. God's hand has been on Ashley's life all along, and I have no doubt that he will continue to direct my friend's steps forward into the next chapter. Suffice it to say, I believe the world needs to hear Ashley's story, and I am humbled and blessed that the Lord saw fit for me to play a small part in it.

As for the rest of our conversation that afternoon, I'll leave it to Brother Ashley to relate. His is a story that can scream out to people who are hurting and meet them in the tear-filled, angry, frustrated, and embarrassed place they are. He didn't know it, but he has often been the "salt" for others—preserving the life in them with a kind word or helping them in some small way, even when he didn't have a lot to give.

So many of us churn and churn, spinning our wheels to worry about self, self, self. Brother Ashley does not. He is a person who knows it's better to give than to receive. So why Ashley? God knew helping him was the shortest path to blessing many others.

Blessings are not meant to be cul-de-sacs; they're supposed to be expressways. We're blessed to be blessings to others. I have been personally blessed to be a blessing—to have played the game of football and conducted myself in a way to have earned the respect of others. It is my honor to use my God-given platform to shine a light on Brother Ashley, to become a blessing to him, and to watch God's faithfulness as he multiplies that blessing across geography and time.

Make no mistake—that's exactly what's happening right now. As you can probably tell, I believe in divine connections and appointments. The fact that you're holding this book is one of them.

The first time Ashley helped someone, the dominoes of blessing in and from his life began to fall. Each time Ashley helped someone, God brought him one step closer to this moment—another divine appointment on the journey of his blessed life. Along the way blessings accumulated, poured back on him, and then rippled outward, reaching people he has never met and likely never will. In fact, you are holding this book because Ashley decided one day to help someone else, and someone else, and someone else.

His story, and therefore this book, is the product of a lifetime of those choices, as all our lives will be.

As you read about Ashley's incredible and blessed life, I hope you remember something: it's no coincidence that you chose to read or listen to this powerful move of God to add to your blessed joy.

Brian Dawkins
Man of God
Blessed by the Best
Pro Football Hall of Fame
Author

NOTE FROM SPONSOR

My friend Ashley Shumba is one of the most enthusiastic, compassionate, and inspiring people I've ever met. His character and life story are an encouraging testimony that good things happen to good people. He equally reinforces my belief in the power of positivity.

Ashley's motivating story resonated with me so deeply that I felt compelled to help him share it with the world. As you'll learn in this book, although his life originates from humble beginnings, his hard work, gratitude, and selflessness guided him to happiness and success.

Our friendship developed organically, and that was meaningful to me. I met Ashley in 2022, when I hired his transportation company to drive my family and me to an event. Immediately, I was impressed by how seriously he took his job and his professionalism. He is regarded as someone who provides the best experience possible for his clients. He takes great pride in the little things, choosing to focus on the details and what he can control. The result is that he always makes travel more enjoyable. He knows precisely how to create wonderful experiences for his clients, and he does so generously and with his whole heart.

In that first meeting, I learned about his journey immigrating from Zimbabwe and all the struggles and challenges he's overcome. Despite those obstacles, he is a rare man—one who is incredibly happy with his life and all the good fortune he has encountered. All this is to say that if you met Ashley, you might never know that he is someone who came from very little and experienced the intervention of fate, over and over and over, to get where he is today. Ashley's warm and respectful spirit, combined with his professionalism and work ethic, also make him easy to get to know and befriend. He possesses a natural exuberance, tenacity, and humility that make people want to be a part of moving his life forward in some substantial, meaningful way.

Ashley drives for me almost exclusively because I enjoy the time we spend together. But I also routinely hire him to drive the many business associates and international professionals I host. Unfailingly, they take me aside afterward.

"Have you heard Ashley's story?" they ask.

"Yes," I answer. "That's exactly why I wanted him to drive you."

His story is simply incredible, and I am honored to play a small part in helping him share it.

Although Ashley and I come from different backgrounds, we have the same principles. I have the pleasure of serving as president of the Philadelphia Insurance Companies Foundation, and that work is the best part of my job. Ashley is a true giver and helper at heart. Whatever he has, he will use to help someone else. That's something I've always tried to do across my personal life, in my relationships, and in my career. It's a belief the two of us share with Pro Football Hall of Famer Brian Dawkins, another person who has had the fortune to befriend Ash. Brian and I have become friends and shared a desire to bring Ash's story to others through this book.

I hope you find as much joy from learning about his journey as I have. Ashley's account shouts that he was destined to have doors opened for him. His pride in doing for others and in being a good person has opened doors that changed the trajectory of his life. All this to say that Ashley uses the qualities that make up his rare, wonderful character—his exuberance, affability, tenacity, humility, integrity, and yes, his goodness—to make his own luck.

His appreciation and celebration of his where he is today—a US citizen, a husband, and a father to three beautiful children—all highlight that working hard and being nice to people pays off. I believe that in the end, if you're a good person and you live your life, work hard, and care about the little things, good fortune will come to you and from you. If I hadn't believed it before, Ashley's life would have convinced me of that truth.

After you read his memoir, I think you'll see why. And along with so many others, you'll learn just how easy it is to celebrate Ashley himself.

John W. Glomb Jr.
President
Philadelphia Insurance Companies Foundation

The Limo Ride that Changed My Life

I was on my way to church when I got the call that would change my life.

As one of the top twenty highest paid chauffeurs in the United States, I have come in contact with many celebrities, dignitaries, and all manner of people. Sometimes I've been aware of who they are, other times not. American celebrities are not always known in Africa, and although I immigrated to the States in 2012, I still cross paths with individuals I don't know are famous. That's especially true when it comes to celebrated American football players.

On that fateful day, I received a call from my workmate based in Philadelphia. It was my usual day off, but he asked me to do an airport pickup. A football player, he said. Very VIP. I was to collect him at Philadelphia International Airport and drive him to his hotel. I agreed to take on the job. Yes, it was my day off, but I've always been a go-getter. Truth be told, I wasn't a fan of American football at the time, so I just took it as a normal drive. I went home, donned my suit, and left to pick up the limousine I'd be driving.

A few hours later, I arrived at Philadelphia International Airport and navigated my limo to the arrivals area. My phone rang—my contact for the pickup.

"I'm the coordinator for the Philadelphia Eagles," he said, by way of introduction. I strained to hear him over the airport traffic. "The gentleman you're picking up is at the airport waiting for you."

"Thank you, sir."

He repeated the name of the person I was there to chauffeur, and I was certain he called the man Gail. We ended the call, and I began scanning the area, looking for my pickup.

Nothing.

I pulled up to curb after curb, rolled down my window, repeating the same question.

"Are you Gail?" I asked, over and over, always to the same response.

"Nope."

Meanwhile, seconds turned into minutes. Wherever Gail was, his wait was growing longer with each passing moment. I was starting to sweat. My pickup had been scheduled for four thirty in the afternoon, and I was almost an hour late.

Finally, I called my company back in desperation. "What does this guy look like?" I asked.

At the other end of the line, my colleague, Michael Tracy, started cracking up.

"Brain Dawkins?" he said, laughing. "Former player for the Philadelphia Eagles? Pro Football Hall of Famer? Look for the tall guy—the one being followed around by people asking him to pose for selfies. That'll be him."

All this time I'd been looking for *Gail*. That was unfortunate.

I took another pass around the area, this time looking for a

INTRODUCTION

crowd. Finally! There he was: a heavily built, muscular man right in the middle of a group of people asking for autographs and posing for pictures—on the other side of the arrivals area. He looked frustrated and tired.

It took me another fifteen minutes to maneuver my limousine to where he stood. I parked, jumped out of the car, and began apologizing for my tardiness. Celebrity or no, I prided myself on prompt, on-time pickups. "I didn't know what you looked like," I explained.

Truthfully, I knew I should've done my research first. My colleagues had emphasized that he was popular. I could've googled him and seen a photo. I felt embarrassed about the oversight, so I kept apologizing. But all the apologies in the world couldn't change the fact that he had spent an hour stranded on the curb, surrounded by fans while waiting for me. He was exhausted and, understandably, deeply frustrated to the point that he wouldn't even allow me the chance to take his bag or open the car door for him.

"I'm sorry this happened," I said again. "Please don't think I'm ignorant, but I don't know who you are. Football isn't popular in my home country."

I knew it wasn't a good start. Nevertheless, we settled in for the ride. "By the way, my name is Ashley Shumba," I said.

"Nice meeting you, Ashley," he responded, his voice calm. "I'm Brian Dawkins, former pro American football player."

As we made our way from the chaos of the airport and toward the distant Philadelphia skyline, I asked Mr. Dawkins more about American football. He explained that he had retired as a player and was now operations executive for the Eagles football club. Eventually, the temperature of the conversation warmed.

"You have a beautiful accent," he said after a while. (I would later learn that he'd recognized it was African the moment I began talking to him.) "Where are you from?"

"A small village in Zimbabwe."

"Tell me something," he said. "I've heard that it's hard to get a visa to come to America."

"That's true."

"Most of the time, you have to be a doctor or a scientist."

"Yes." And I'd seen my fair share of them leave the visa office empty-handed.

"But you're driving a limousine," he pointed out. "How did you qualify? It must've been very hard for you."

"My story is unique," I admitted. After all, I had lived, visited, and worked in Angola, Botswana, Canada, England, Egypt, France, Germany, the Netherlands, Switzerland, South Africa, Lesotho, Namibia, Tanzania, Kenya, the United Arab Emirates, Zambia, my home country of Zimbabwe, and now, the United States—quite literally all over the world. I hadn't known anyone in America when I immigrated here in 2012, but I believed in my personal strengths and abilities. My story is one of unexpected opportunities and unforeseen recognition, of hardship and unrealized dreams and incredible victories.

"I've been fortunate my entire life," I added.

When we finally reached Mr. Dawkins's hotel, he didn't move to get out of the car.

"Can you pull over?" he asked.

One thing I've come to learn about America is that there are people here with love in their hearts. There are people here who will care enough to take someone from the street—who is at the lowest point in their life—and raise him up.

I pulled the car over as Mr. Dawkins said the words that would change my life:

"I want to hear your story."

A NEW DREAM

Mr. Dawkins and I sat in that limousine for an hour as I narrated the story of my life. By the end, our conversation was flowing naturally; all of Mr. Dawkins's earlier frustration seemed to have vanished. I wondered why.

"Look—I want to get real with you," he said.

My first thought was that he meant our initial misunderstanding—my late arrival and his hour-long wait. I admitted as much and was surprised by his answer.

"No," he said. "I'm thinking of changing your life. I had to work so hard to create my success. But I see that you have this . . . blessing around you. God has made way after way for you. I think there's a powerful message in your life story that people need to hear."

Even then, I knew anyone could have listened to my story and said, "I'm just going to get the rights to that," and move on. But Mr. Dawkins didn't want to own my story. He wanted to *share* it with the world. And he wanted to help lift me up.

I was amazed that this person in front of me could go from frustrated to positive so quickly—that he could grasp that positivity and dream of ways it could benefit others. But then again, I tend to have that effect on people.

Right then and there, he proposed that I write a book—*this* book. We discussed it, and afterward, he prayed for me and asked God to give us strength for the project. I realized he has a strong faith and felt he was godsent. He had also confided in me his hope of taking this book to Hollywood and turning it into a film.

Hollywood. After hearing my story, he knew what that word would mean to me.

CHAPTER 1
Humble Beginnings—
My Childhood in Mberengwa, Zimbabwe

I n this life, we are all blessed with talents. Whether we use them or not is another story. For my part, I was always athletic. I ran short distances, usually one hundred meters. I was always the number one or number two on my team throughout high school. Sometimes I regret that I didn't pursue that talent, but it gave me another chance to develop my leadership skills. It always seemed that no matter where I was, or what group I was with, I was always in charge.

There aren't a lot of resources in Africa, but one group I was part of managed to exert our creativity to wire together a motor vehicle. I was ten years old at the time, putting batteries together, building a car that was small and light enough to carry us over distances. When my parents found out about it, they said I was going to be an engineer.

"You have a gift," they said.

But what they saw as a gift for electrical systems was really a gift of creativity. I always knew that, and I knew I could use it in more ways than just stringing together batteries and wires.

Looking back, I recognize that I grew up in a village that simply didn't have the infrastructure for recognizing and identifying gifts in children. The adults in my village were too focused on feeding their families to concern themselves with creativity. But I often wonder what might have happened if I had been born elsewhere, perhaps in America, where that infrastructure did exist. Who would I have become? It wasn't until much later in my life—when I was eighteen—that someone saw the unique creativity in me.

But there, in my childhood, I was focused on one thing: selling vegetables and beverages during the drought season, on behalf of my neighbor.

YOUNG ENTREPRENEUR

There is a photograph of me as a child from the year 1984, when I was seven years old. I am wearing my school uniform—tan shorts and a button-down, short-sleeved shirt. I'm standing in my village of Mberengwa, Zimbabwe, on a dirt road, in what I call "the ghetto." The photo stops at my ankles. If my feet hadn't been cropped out, anyone would see that they were bare.

That wasn't uncommon at my village school where no one wore shoes. The reason for that was simple—none of us owned any. That same year, Zimbabwe was experiencing a deadly civil war and, simultaneously, experiencing its worst drought in recorded history. Over one million livestock in my country had died, and it was tough to get a decent meal.

But I have always thought that in life, you will either step forward into growth or you will step back into safety. Even at age seven, I chose to step forward and become a young entrepreneur.

I didn't think of "entrepreneurship" at the time, of course; I simply followed my instincts to move forward and look for opportunities that would come my way. The drought was horrible, but the hardships it caused also gave me the strength to keep going.

So at seven years of age, I began working for a white man who taught at the local high school. I sold fruits, beverages, and vegetables in the streets of my village on his behalf. In return, he taught me about finance and how to save money. By the end of that year, I had saved the equivalent of fifty US dollars—a small fortune. I surprised my mum with the money and told her to use it to buy food.

Attending school during the drought and civil war, keeping up with my studies, and trying to make money to help my parents all the while wasn't easy. A lot of us in my village matured early; we saw the worst side of the world at a tender age. Still, I don't regret the experience. It made me more ambitious. It made me a go-getter. It gave me the foundation of entrepreneurial skills that have served me well throughout my life.

The white man was also the person who took that photograph of me. I've kept it ever since, and I'm happy to have it. It inspires me to keep going, to keep being ambitious, to keep working hard. I'll show it to my own children when they're old enough and tell them where their father came from—and how fortunate we are to be here.

UNSPOILING

I was a hard worker, but I was also the youngest in my family— the baby. Perhaps I was coddled more because of it. I think my father saw that. As I got older, he decided I had too many friends around to distract me. And perhaps he was right. In truth, I often acted the fool a little bit and let my marks at school slip. I wasn't performing as well as I could have.

Unbeknownst to me, my father had devised a solution. He saved the money, and he kept saving, secretly, with my mom. Why? So that they could send me to Mnene Boarding School.

I was ten years old when they informed me of their plan and assured me I would be attending a very good school. That "very good school," however, was many hours away—the equivalent of traveling from New York to New Jersey. On the day of my departure, they packed a small bag of my belongings, gave me money for the journey, and put me on a bus.

Alone.

My mother told me I was to change buses twice, meaning it would take three different buses to get me all the way from the village to my new school. She also gave me a warning. At the time, civil war had erupted in my country, so the warning also came with strict instructions.

"You be careful," she said. "If someone asks you to come with them, don't agree. Take your bag and take this bus, then this one, then this one." (Future visits home would involve similar instructions, written in a letter from my mother and accompanied with bus fare, ending with a simple, "I'll see you at home.")

So at the tender age of ten, I hefted my suitcase onto bus after bus after bus and made my way to the boarding school. When I arrived at school, I found the principal and gave him a letter my parents had written that explained who I was and why I had come. "Why did your father think you were ready for boarding school?" the principal exclaimed. "You're so young!"

I cried for a week.

As I would soon learn, I was the youngest student in my class. I felt like I had been abandoned in the jungle, left to awaken at five each morning, take a cold shower, and sweep my dormitory before going to eat a small bowl of porridge at six. Punctual meal-times followed throughout the day: tea at ten, lunch at one in the afternoon, dinner in the evening. It was a very different way of eating than I'd enjoyed at home, and it came to symbolize all the shocking differences I experienced in my new environment. At home, I ate a variety of fruits and other foods whenever I wanted. Boarding school would turn out to be a good thing in my life, but it was tough for a while.

School sessions ran from January to April, and then from mid-May to August, and from mid-September to December. It was so far from my village that I couldn't go home except on those breaks. So beginning at age ten, I had only three months a year with my parents. When I turned thirteen, they sent me to Chegato High School, another boarding school that was governed by the Evangelical Lutheran Church. And that cycle continued—meaning I also spent my entire youth away from my siblings and relatives. Still, those same friends and family members recall how my dad "unspoiled" me at such a tender age.

I still remember coming home from boarding school one day when I was twelve, to the news that my grandmother wasn't feeling well and that I needed to deliver money for her care. But before I could deliver it, I had to pick it up. I traveled the distance of New York to Washington, DC to retrieve the money from an uncle, then traveled another long distance to deliver the money to a second uncle who used it for my grandmother's care. I stayed the night there and took another bus home the following morning to spend the remainder of my break with my family.

BECOMING SELF-SUFFICIENT

I've always thought my father somehow knew that I wanted to be independent and that he did what he could to help me achieve it. Suffice it to say that I was behaving like an adult by age eleven. That meant that when my parents sent me a sum of money to have while I was at school—say, twenty dollars for a term—I knew that money translated into cookies and any other food I wanted. *This is pocket money*, I thought, and I knew just how to make it last.

I took it straight to the principal at my school.

"This is my pocket money," I said. "I want you to hold it for me."

He agreed, and we came up with an arrangement: I would come to him every week and take out a little to buy my own sweets, or something to drink, or what have you. Whatever I didn't spend, I saved, and when I went home on breaks, I deposited my savings in a drawer. I have always been reliable and honest by nature, and I built on the entrepreneurial foundation to save as much as I could—a lesson I'd learned while selling vegetables in my earlier village years.

I became so good at saving money, in fact, that my mom began to rely on the fact that she could borrow from me to buy wood or food. (Houses in Zimbabwe at that time, at least in our village, did not have electricity or running water and thus also required Blair toilets—ventilated pit latrines—to be built outside the house.) She had discovered the drawer in which I kept my money and dipped into it often.

"Can I borrow some money from you?" she'd ask, sometimes taking one dollar, other times five. At that rate, I knew my savings would soon be depleted. *I must open a bank account*, I resolved.

The trick was, I had to do it without my parents' knowledge. But the next time I went to town, I opened that secret bank account and continued saving as much as I could. The bank gave me a small book for recording my deposits and withdrawals, and I kept that a secret, too. Then one day, my father made a discovery while picking up my clothes. He found my bank book and realized right away what it was. "You hid a bank account?" he asked in disbelief. "Yes, because Mama used to take money from the drawer I kept it in," I answered. And that was that.

I continued to build on the financial skills I learned and earned the respect of the adults at my school. They named me a prefect and put me in charge of one hundred other students. I was responsible for monitoring their cleanliness, behavior, and punctuality.

In ways big and small, I trained myself to be reliable, dependable, and honest—especially when it came to money. It was those same skills that would, in a moment of kismet, take me from Africa entirely.

CHAPTER 2

First City, First Love

Although I couldn't have known it at the time, my departure from Africa would begin with a love story.

To get there, I first had to leave the boarding school that had become something like home to me over the last half of my life.

It isn't uncommon for city people to be afraid of rural areas—and vice versa. People like to know what to expect, so the unfamiliar can be unsettling. For my part, I was used to the deep, comforting darkness of night in rural areas. I have always found it serene and peaceful. With that feeling, I moved into town for the first time when I was eighteen years old. A new resident of Harare, Zimbabwe, I ate my very first restaurant meal and saw my very first four-way traffic lights. But instead of feeling unsettled by all the change, I felt . . . electrified.

Everything was new to me; I found it all fascinating. Everywhere I looked were young people—not much older than me—dressed in suits and driving cars. Can you imagine what that was like for a boy from a small village and boarding school?

I admired them from a distance, wondering what their lives had been like. What had led them to the moment they slipped on their first tailored jacket or sat down behind the wheel? Without realizing it, I had entered my own love story.

TO BE OR NOT TO BE . . . AN ARTIST

I had fallen irrevocably in love with the arts industry. My love began early in my youth, when I was at boarding school. I used to read what I thought of as Hollywood magazines and through them learned to admire actors like Denzel Washington, Eddie Murphy, and Tom Cruise. Their careers tugged at my heart, and I was enthralled by the lifestyles they led. At some point I began imagining that I, too, was a successful producer or actor in Hollywood—one that others looked up to as a role model. I dreamed of leveraging my success in Hollywood to help develop my community.

Once that dream took root, it never left me. I grew so focused and dedicated to achieving it that my uncles used to call me "Mr. Hollywood." And in so many ways, I felt like Mr. Hollywood. Deep within me was a certainty that I would one day wind up in America, pursuing my shining showbiz dreams.

Being born in the environment I had been born in was tricky, and it gave me a great many obstacles to overcome. Still, I remained committed. My entire family and all my friends knew I had fallen hard for Hollywood, that I was crazily in love with the arts. Everything I did was in pursuit of my dream of movies and going to America. But in Harare, I tried a dozen times to audition, but with no luck. I was never even hired to be in an ensemble.

After so many "nos," why did I keep hearing that still, small voice inside that told me I would make it? To this day, I don't know. All I can say is that it was a constant reminder, fanning the flame of my inspiration to try harder, keep going, and do more. It gave me the perseverance and will to infuse my journey through life with change.

So I kept knocking on doors. From one film office to the next, I knocked. From one "no" to the next, I kept knocking. Then one day in 1996, I knocked on the right door.

I met Ross Mackam, a white man who took pity on me and introduced me to a theatrical musical director named Dawn Parkinson. To my great delight, Dawn hired me as an extra for the musical *Blood Brothers*.

During rehearsals, I met another man, Mr. Ian McVey. Ian already had several assistant director credits to his name in Hollywood, and he recognized the passion in me to do more than perform. Ian always believed in my dreams, and he started motivating me to come up with my own projects. Before long, I set my sights on a production of my own.

I had imagined a production as a simple process, but I lacked funding—and that meant it proved to be the exact opposite. But for all the funding I lacked, I had enormous amounts of the thing that really mattered.

Motivation. The kind that burns deep down in the soul. That kind of motivation is rare. Most people don't have it, but thankfully, I did.

My desire to be a director or producer grew inside me, both fueled by the burn of my motivation and stoking its fire. I went from company to company, seeking support, but to no avail. Then one day in 1997, Mr. and Mrs. Rob Standish-White, a couple I'd met during the *Blood Brothers* production, gave me a soft loan of a few hundred dollars to start a small theater group with drop-out students. I was twenty years old.

I began hiring my actors, designing my production, and engaging a venue. Rehearsals began shortly after. By that time I had also become involved in all disciplines of the arts, from promotion and managing small musical groups to producing world-class pageants and fashion shows, complete with corporate sponsorship. Sponsorships were especially uncommon at that time in Africa, and entertainment was generally not well funded. What money could be given was usually swept up in the fight against the HIV/AIDS epidemic, poverty challenges, and political instability.

A few weeks into rehearsals, something unexpected happened. My plucky group and I began drawing attention from the media—a lot of attention. Reporters were fascinated by the fact that someone as young as me had the ability to obtain funding from globally recognized brands and navigate the diplomatic community.

As you can imagine, I felt the pressure of that to the core of my being. I poured even more time and energy into the production. Alas, I reached the bottom of my funding long before the run of my show was scheduled to end and was ultimately forced to cancel most of the performances. I was deeply frustrated. Why did I have that fire in me to produce and direct, if only to watch the dream slip through my fingers?

At the time, I was living with my uncle, Biriam Wabatagore, who was a successful lawyer, and his wife, Audrey Kadungure-Wabatagore, who, in those days, was a high school teacher. Biriam witnessed my frustration and rallied behind me, giving me hope and encouraging me to never give up when I needed it most. "Let the risks and the rewards keep you going," he always said.

At one point, I remembered Shakespeare and drew courage from *Hamlet*: "To be or not to be; that is the question. Whether 'tis nobler in the mind to suffer the slings and arrows outrageous fortune, or to take arms against a sea of troubles, and by opposing them?"

If Hamlet could oppose a sea of troubles, then so could I. Gathering my metaphorical arms in Shakespearean fashion, I recommitted myself to that great battle against outrageous fortune. I would stand strong against a sea of monetary troubles. I would find my path forward and walk it.

Meanwhile, conflict in my family was brewing. In my hometown, my parents had grown increasingly disappointed with the lack of tangible success from my career in the arts. They insisted, with increasing frequency and vehemence, that I return to school. Again and again, I refused.

My uncle, who had witnessed my initial failure and frustration, continued to fight for me. One day, he and my parents had an . . . exchange. Their words grew more and more passionate. I suppose, in their way, they were each fighting for what they thought was best for me. But in the end, my uncle had the last word.

"Ashley is living in my house," he said, "and I have every right to give him a chance to try out his career of interest. *Stay out of this.*"

And that was that.

For my part, I continued to hustle. All I needed was a breakthrough—one financial backer, one open door, one person with the kind of connections I needed to extend their hand.

It wasn't happening. I prayed. I cried. I hustled harder than I ever had in my entire life. And still, things weren't working out. I had fallen so deeply in love with the arts. Why hadn't the industry fallen in love with me?

FIRE TO FRUSTRATION

In my life, I've learned the wisdom of surrounding yourself with successful people. From them, it's possible to learn from their experience and gain insights into what it takes to be successful. They can also help you network.

In 1997, Oliver Mtukudzi—the world-renowned Afro Jazz and Tuku Music artist—was in town to give a performance at the

French Embassy in Harare. I met him at an event, and for reasons I still don't know, he gave me his telephone number. I quickly fell into a routine of calling him each morning. Sometimes he would beat me to the call; my phone would ring, and there was Oliver on the other end of the line, inviting me to accompany him to an event.

He even invited me to be a curtain raiser before his performance at the French Embassy. For those who aren't in the entertainment industry, a curtain raiser is the opening act before a major performance.

A few minutes before the curtain went up on Oliver's performance at the embassy, I gave a solo dance. Being onstage was exhilarating, and I couldn't deny that something inside me clicked. There was a *rightness* in those moments of footwork and muscle movement and rhythm that I had never before experienced. To this day, I don't think I could have experienced it in any other way.

I finished my performance, sweating and happy and fulfilled. If my insides could've burst out in utter joy, I think they would have. I left the stage with something that felt like new purpose. Like a new dawn, breaking over me. In my heart, the fire raged.

Immediately afterward, I was approached by the French ambassador. I had impressed him with my dance, he said. The next thing I knew, he offered to facilitate a scholarship for me to go to France and study dance and music.

My appearance onstage with Oliver opened many doors for me. Even more importantly, he became my mentor. Through all those early morning calls and events—at which he always introduced me as his little brother—he always encouraged me to remain focused. Determined. "Whatever your heart desires," he repeated often, "you have to put on your mind. Your determination will always prevail."

He may have introduced me as his little brother, but in my eyes, he was a father figure. By that point, he had entered a new era of success in his own artistic career. For my part, I simply savored the opportunity to bond with someone I respected and admired so much. Even now, it amazes me that our bond was such that each time I told him I was traveling, he gifted me with "pocket money." I appreciated the gesture more than words can express, of course. But even more meaningful to me were the introductions he made between me and other celebrities, corporate successes, and promoters. He always hoped I would have a breakthrough in show business. But for all of his help and mentorship, I still wasn't breaking through.

Late in the year 1998, I woke up early one December morning and went into town. I was still heartsick over my nonstarter of a career, and, despite my best Shakespearian efforts, I'd begun to question and doubt. I also found myself thinking about my friends' lives. They were in college and doing well; I was still loitering in the capital city with nothing to my name, unsure of what to do next. I knelt down and cried out to God. "Why have you forgotten me?" I asked.

But of course, God had done no such thing.

CHAPTER 3
London Calling

A t eight o'clock one morning in December of 1998, I found myself walking down First Street Road in the city center of Harare, Zimbabwe. I was still discouraged, still wondering what to do next. I vividly remember the feel of early morning air on my skin, the scent of city streets in my nostrils, the sound of my steps on the road as I continued to put one foot in front of the other. Despite my discouragement, my heart reveled in those small, simple details of city life—even as I was approached by a gentleman I didn't recognize.

"Excuse me," he said in English, his accent distinctly British. "Where might I find the National Arts Council of Zimbabwe?"

"It's three blocks that way," I said, pointing. But Harare is a lot like New York in that it's teeming with people. The man looked slightly discouraged.

"Can you take me there?" he asked.

"I'll walk with you," I agreed.

We chatted amiably along the way. He introduced himself as Bilaal Ameen and told me about his mission in my country: to handpick a group of ten young people that would travel with him to Europe as a theater and dance group. Together, they would travel England, France, and the Netherlands for four weeks, exchanging their skills and culture with each other and their audiences. Bilaal's endeavor was sponsored by the British Arts Council and the European Commission. They were looking for experienced artists who, upon completion of the exchange project, would return home and work closely with United Nations Educational, Scientific, and Cultural Organization to implement charitable projects in their respective countries.

For a moment, I allowed myself to dream about what that would be like—to see places I'd only read about in school, to taste their food, to speak with their people. And to breathe the air of London, the home of Shakespeare himself! I could picture myself there.

In my mind the dream felt so real, as if I'd turned a page and stepped into the beginning of something special. Joining Bilaal's group would be utterly magical. Without any permission from me, my heart yearned for the experience. But I quickly reconciled that the opportunity couldn't be for me. Bilaal told me that the program was open to people who were theatre practitioners. I was still an amateur and too young to have gained any experience.

THERE CAN BE MIRACLES

Bilaal and I reached the National Arts Council building and entered together. I found myself determined to make sure he spoke to the right person. Even if I couldn't be a part of his program, I wanted that life-changing experience for the people Bilaal had come to seek out. I asked to speak with the Director of the National Arts Council, Mr. Titus Chipangura.

"This gentleman is looking for youths to go to Europe on an exchange project," I said in my home language when the director appeared. I explained the details Bilaal had related to me on our walk. Then I made introductions and left the room. But something in me urged me to wait in the lobby, just in case. After all, Bilaal might need more assistance finding his way around the streets of Harare.

I spent the next stretch of time looking at the furniture while the office's sounds filled my ears. I wondered whom Bilaal would choose to join his troupe of artists and was glad that I played a small, anonymous part in helping them have the experience.

The next thing I knew, the director popped his head around the corner.

"Ashley," he said, waving me back into his office, "do you have a passport?"

"No."

I'd never had a reason to get one, and I knew they could be notoriously difficult to obtain—not to mention, they were expensive.

"You're going to need one," the director informed me. "This gentleman wants you to join his group as one of the ten artists."

I was stunned into silence.

"You've been so helpful," Bilaal said, a warm smile lighting his features. "Showing me around, bringing me here, and interceding on my behalf—I can't thank you enough."

"It takes three days to process an emergency passport," the director continued, plowing past the pleasantries. "I'll help you with that."

Not only would I need an emergency passport, but I would also need a very specific visa (known as a Schengen visa) that allowed me to travel through multiple countries in Europe. We wouldn't only be traveling to England, France, and the Netherlands, but also—*also!*— through Belgium, Switzerland, Sweden, and others.

I would soon learn that the director had bigger plans than just helping me obtain a passport and visa. He had also decided to pay part of my hefty passport fee.

"I'm going back to Britain next week," Bilaal said, pulling me back into the moment. "I'll send documentation to your house and require you to visit the British Airways offices to pick up the tickets for the group."

Again, I was stunned. I was only twenty-one—not even old enough to join the group. And yet, there I was, suddenly finding myself in charge of something so important.

When Bilaal approached me on the street, I couldn't have known he was heaven-sent. But there he was, smiling and opening that door, extending a hand full of dreams and inviting me to take them. For a few long moments, I couldn't believe it.

That dream I had longed for.

Everything I had wished, yearned, and prayed for.

In two months, it would be my reality.

It felt like a real, tangible miracle. Imagine—to meet someone on the street and then, an hour later, be a part of a group that would tour Europe. I was giddy. I remembered the scholarship the French ambassador had arranged for me the previous year—I had the funding already in place. Bilaal and I arranged to speak again, and at the first opportunity I rushed off to tell my uncle and his wife.

As one might imagine, Biriam and Audrey were incredibly happy for me. With God's help, my perseverance had produced fruit. The fire in me had put me in a place of possibility. My uncle and aunt called everyone in the family to break the good news, and I thanked them for believing in and supporting me. My uncle even paid the rest of my passport fees.

I realized something that day: doing good in life makes the whole family proud. My personal success was a Shumba family success. With that realization, I embarked on the next chapter of my story. I was the only member of the group with a strong rural background and, of course, the youngest of them all. But just like them, I would leave my home country the following month for the dazzle of a European tour.

In the meantime, I began rehearsals for cultural dances to present alongside renowned artists like Tsungai Garise (artistic director), Albert Mkunzi, Sandra Chidawanyika, Patricia Mabviko, Charles Chiyangwa, Yohane Weseni, and others.

In *Europe*.

EYE-OPENING EXPERIENCES

Before I left for the tour, my whole family gathered around me to wish me luck and celebrate this success. Being included in the group of artists had even garnered media attention—everyone else in the tour came from different cities, so it was something of a big deal that I had been selected from Harare.

My parents took me aside before I left. "We want you to be successful," they said, "but we are worried that you won't come back."

"I'm going to come back," I promised. After all, the mission of the tour required me to.

"Let him go," my uncle said. And they did.

When we finally set out for our tour, I knew I was about to see new things and have new experiences. I would see the Eiffel Tower; I would fly on an airplane for the first time and stay in hotels. What I couldn't have understood then, however, was how new all the small things making up my day-to-day life would be.

Take, for instance, visiting the Eiffel Tower. Until we left England to see it, I'd had no idea that it was possible to move from Britain to France through something called the English Channel. I had just moved from a small African village; those kinds of details had never been part of my experience.

Neither was air travel, for that matter. I've enjoyed many good laughs through the years remembering what happened on my first flight, when we all had to buckle our safety belts. I didn't know what to do, and somehow, I managed to almost choke myself. And then later, in my first hotel room, a friend had to help me turn on the water.

It was all so new to me, but I enjoyed every second and quickly adapted. And not long after our arrival in England, the office of the mayor of the City of London hosted a welcome dinner for us. Just imagine: twelve young people from Africa, touring extensively throughout England, France, and the Netherlands, visiting cities often considered, in one way or another, birthplaces of culture and art. It was an amazing opportunity.

And for me, opportunity was just beginning.

CHAPTER 4
The White-Collar Dream

Returning home to Zimbabwe after my traveling through Europe, I found that the trip had opened a lot of doors for me, both personally and professionally. Not only was I able to call all my fellow artists friends (and still do today), but upon my return I was hired by the Harare International Festival of Arts to serve as a venue manager. My chance to implement all the rich lessons I'd learned while traveling was at hand.

I was twenty-two at the time and the youngest manager on record for the festival. I knew that if I wanted to rise through the ranks, I had much still to learn. But I was willing and eager to put in the work. The fire in me had only risen since my travels, and I recognized that my colleagues were people who had worked at the festival for a while. They were much more experienced than me. My title might have been *manager*, but I privately designated myself as a student as well. I was determined to learn everything I could from those around me.

Perhaps as a result, I made tremendous contacts through the festival—contacts who helped me implement other projects without any problems. I enjoyed my time at the event, but my focus remained firmly on becoming a successful producer and director. As I worked, my vision continued to take shape.

My new job felt like the first step in the right direction. I began wearing shiny suits and a confident look; I entered the morning rush every day. Before long, I also began to see a steady, lucrative income rolling my way.

I sometimes thought of the young people I'd first admired when I was new to Harare—the ones skillfully driving through the crush of traffic lights, other cars, and pedestrians. Like them, I had entered a new normal—what I thought of as the white-collar dream. I liked it—a lot—and had every intention of making that dream my reality. For good.

BUILDING FROM THE GROUND UP

In the year 2001, I came up with the idea to produce a pageant. I decided it wouldn't be just any run-of-the-mill beauty pageant. There would be that element, of course, but it would also be a humanitarian effort. My goal was to bring less privileged young women of African origin to my country. I dreamed of the moment when the world could see African people coming together in a spirit of oneness.

But I needed an office. At that time, I didn't have one. After the festival, I'd moved on to work as an independent producer. I'd made remarkable contacts, including sponsors who offered to bankroll my projects. Remembering that, I thought of my old friend Mr. Ian McVey, from the *Blood Brothers* production. Mr. McVey was the director of a multi-million-dollar company called Hunting Industries. He was doing ads for a theater and asked me to meet him at a golf club to volunteer as an extra for an advertisement being filmed there.

On the day of the shoot, I met Mr. McVey at the golf club. Looking around at all the production staff and actors, I took note that I was the youngest person there. But while other actors taking part in the production were being paid for their work, I was only volunteering. Before long, Mr. McVey began talking to me about how to increase my chances of being hired as a paid actor for ads. "It's a good profession," he said. "I want to teach you. Here's my credit card. Go inside and buy drinks for everyone."

I happened to be the only Black person at the white-owned club. I entered with a list of drinks and walked up to the counter where another guy was already perched on a seat next to me. "Are you part of the production taking place?" he asked. "What are you doing? This?"

He gestured to the bar and the drinks.

"No, I'm an extra," I answered, looking at all the different bottles and beverages and wondering how everything went together. "I've been sent in to buy drinks."

"Let me help you."

He began to describe all the different alcohols and what went with them. For my part, I learned things like *this can't be just orange juice* and *that needs some spirits to go with it*. With his help, I rounded up all the drinks on the list and took them back out to the production team.

Things were going well enough. However, at that point my English vocabulary wasn't good, and I'd been mixing up my mother language in my attempts at English. But somehow, that didn't stop Mr. McVey from wanting to keep helping me.

"I would like you to come to my office," he said, when I had successfully delivered the drinks he'd requested, "so I can hear your presentation."

I'd been telling him my idea for the pageant, and I was thrilled he wanted to hear more.

"You need to start acting like a businessperson," he cautioned me. "You cannot wear these vibrantly colored T-shirts in the meetings. They're good for going to a club, but not appropriate for a business setting."

I nodded my agreement. But what *was* I to wear? A short time later, Mr. McVey took me to a shop. He told me to find three different suits that I could wear in professional settings—only suits in neutral colors, he emphasized, like black and gray. He paid for all three.

"Whenever you go to a meeting, wear one of these suits," he instructed.

I was grateful for Mr. McVey's mentorship, and I learned a lot from him about professionalism. His company kept offices in Harare, and eventually I decided to approach him with a request: Could he afford to lend me a working space at his company?

Mr. McVey surprised me by asking me to come to the office and speak to the board of directors. Right away, I recognized a crucial fact: the board meeting was a test.

Soon a meeting of the board was convened by Ms. Margaret Richards, a member of the company who had taken it upon herself to beg everyone to give me a chance to be a successful young producer.

Before the meeting took place, Mr. McVey explained that I would have an opportunity to speak. "You'll be on your own to convince them," he'd said, "and to do that you'll have to speak like a professional about what is in your heart and what you want from life."

On the day of the meeting, I walked into the meeting room to find Mr. McVey; Mr. Ford, a director; and Mr. Hacker, a chairman.

"This boy has potential," Mr. McVey said to the group gathered around the conference table, "but he doesn't have an office. He doesn't have a cell phone. Could we allow him to use the little room where we normally do our printing? He can use that as an office space and receive calls there. Margaret can direct calls to him and help boost his appearance as a professional." He explained my idea for the pageant, voiced his support, and concluded with a final appeal. "Companies will not give him funding if they see him running his business from a briefcase."

He turned to me expectantly. It was my turn to speak.

"I think I have a natural ability and talent," I began, "but I lack resources. I'm not looking for money or asking you for it. But I am looking for administrative assistance as I seek funding for my business."

"Where will you get the money?" someone asked.

"Once I have an office to operate from, I'll look for the money myself from nongovernmental organizations and the corporate world."

"He certainly has confidence," one of the men said with a good-natured chuckle. "But what if you don't get the money?"

"I don't believe I won't get the money," I said. "Everything I am doing is based on honesty. It's based on promoting young people and changing their lives. Others will want to help me. They will come aboard. Just try me and see if I fail. I won't."

It was the first time anyone had ever asked them to consider providing an office space for someone who wasn't part of their company. Why would they want to donate company resources like that?

There were two hours of discussion, two hours of going back and forth over my request and the company's needs. Allowing me to use company resources would set a precedent. Not only that, but what was the value for them in making what was essentially a donation to my career? This was a company with resources comparable to some of the largest companies in the world, like Coca-Cola. As far as I had seen, its executives only traveled in private airplanes that flew in and out of private airports. *Who was I*, I thought, *to make such a request?*

I explained my passion to them the best I could. I told them more about my dreams and goals. At one point, I was brought to tears. In the end, everyone voted in my favor. The office was mine to use.

DON'T GIVE ME MONEY

Enter my old nemesis: funding. Or, more specifically, the *need* for funding and the lack of it.

The office space at Mr. McVey's company was an immense help to me because I had a place from which to work and to receive guests and potential sponsors. But each week, the men who had granted me use of the space would come and check on me.

"How's it going?" they would ask.

How it was going was that I didn't yet have anything to show for all my hard work—and all their generosity. They were cheering me on, but I desperately wanted to show them how right they were to invest in me. In fact, I was determined. And in the back of my mind, I held a dollar amount that I thought they might expect me to get.

Day after day, I worked toward that first sponsorship—making calls, asking for introductions, honing my presentation, and hearing "no."

By that point, I had already contacted fourteen sub-Saharan African embassies accredited to Harare and invited them to partner with me on the project. Would they assist me in scouting the most qualified girls from their respective countries? Every single embassy agreed. I then approached African airlines that flew into Zimbabwe with a request for sponsorship. Would they provide one ticket for the girl who was chosen to represent their nation in this worthy and prestigious event? Again, I received an enthusiastic "yes" from each company I asked.

Thus encouraged, I requested a meeting with executives from Coca-Cola to ask for a cash sponsorship. At the meeting, I met a wonderful woman named Lillian Mbayiwa.

"You came to our offices at the right time," she said. "We have funds available to donate. You are such a good man with such a good vision for the future. I have no doubt you will do great things."

She asked for my company bank account details and promised to deposit a generous sponsorship. And just like that, my production was being sponsored by one of the top companies in the world.

I left Coca-Cola's offices smiling and walked outside to a nearby bus stop. The bus arrived; I climbed aboard. I chose a seat beside a beautiful woman, and right away she saw that I was happy.

"My name is Ashley Shumba," I said.

"I'm Lena Kandemwa," she answered. "Why are you so excited? Will you share your good news?"

I told her what had just happened at Coca-Cola. She congratulated me with a smile.

"I work as a secretary for a cellphone company called Firstel," she added. "I know our company also sponsors activities like yours. Would you like to come in tomorrow morning and speak with our director?"

Can you imagine? I readily agreed. The next morning, Lena greeted me with a hug at the company's stunning offices.

"Have a seat, Ash," she said. "You look handsome. I like your suit. I told Mr. Blessing Ndoro about you, and he will see you shortly."

My conversation with Mr. Ndoro was fruitful. He offered to provide a cash prize for the pageant winners in exchange for mentioning his company as a sponsor in all our publications. It was a remarkable moment. After the meeting, I graciously thanked Lena, who was quickly becoming a good friend. We've remained friends ever since.

Finally, it had happened! My first sponsor, Coca-Cola, sent a check. Only, it wasn't for the modest sum I'd imagined. It was for *four times* that amount. I couldn't have been more thrilled, and I immediately ran to show Mr. Ford, Mr. Hacker, and Mr. McVey. "I got a sponsorship," I said. Although they had always been supportive, they too were shocked by the dollar amount.

And they weren't the only ones. Word of my large sponsorship had gotten around, and before long, even journalists were asking me for interviews.

I then went to Alliance Francaise, based in Harare, and asked if they would sponsor the venue, knowing this is what would allow me to launch my pageant. To my great excitement, they agreed. I invited fifty top companies to the launch, and ten of the invitees became my major sponsors: Coca-Cola, Firstel Cellular, Crowne Plaza Hotel, Air Malawi, TAAG-Angola Airlines, Air Tanzania, Air Botswana, the City of Harare, Botswana High Commission, and Zambezi Airlines.

The event gained a lot of attention from the media and the corporate world as so many individuals and companies came on board to sponsor the event. One morning I received a call from a woman named Kiki Divaris, who was serving as chairman of the Miss Zimbabwe pageant. Kiki was well respected in Zimbabwe and well connected to the diplomatic community, and I was honored when she asked me to be the chief judge at the pageant. I also received a call from a gentleman named David Peech who picked up my story from a press release. Mr. Peech was a wealthy man whose family owned over a hundred racing horses. He contacted me to ask how he could help with my event, either in kind or in cash. Mr. Peech's wife was a fashion guru.

Ultimately, the pageant was so successful that the media began speculating that someone was behind my efforts and pushing me forward. Everyone knew what I was doing wasn't easy and assumed a corporation—or even the government—was pulling strings on my behalf from behind the scenes. But the whole time, it was only me—an independent individual continuing to work hard, with the hope and belief in my heart that success was always on its way. Yes, I had developed skills along the way—my theater background had turned me into a very good orator, and people liked my confidence. I am a bit realistic when it comes to overcoming obstacles, but I always go forward with confidence. I truly never doubted that I was going to find the help and money I needed.

And the thing about money is, it's just money. Nothing more and nothing less. If my life is any proof, money has a way of showing up when it's needed. *I'll get money somewhere*, I thought while searching for sponsorships. And I wasn't wrong—not by a long shot.

I couldn't have known it then, but that belief would lead me to tell a beloved and respected member of the NFL the same thing. "I'll get the money," I told Brian Dawkins. And I did.

But that part of the story comes later.

I don't say any of this to brag about myself. Far from it. I say it for anyone holding this book with a dream in their heart. Work hard, appreciate the people around you, and believe in that dream and your ability to achieve it. I can promise you it will take you farther than you could ever imagine.

MENTORS ALL AROUND ME

Mr. McVey taught me so much about how to run a business and how to really talk to people. He was the one who explained to me the nuances of language and how important they could be.

From him I learned how to show respect to a businessperson by addressing them as *sir*, *Ms.*, or another title, and only calling them by their first name when I'd gotten to know them. To Western readers, perhaps that seems like a small thing—something you've always known to do. But to me, it was a revelation. It was one more brick removed from the wall between me and moving forward with my dreams.

I'll also never forget something Mr. McVey told me. "Ash," he said, "when you get your dreams in life, always remember that there's someone in your village who needs help. Always. Don't run away from doing charity work, no matter how much money you make. Buy your cars, your homes, all the things that you want. But save money for charity. *Leave room in your heart for charity.*"

I was so young when he told me that. And still, I think it's such a big part of why I succeeded so early in life because it had such a profound influence on the way I think about success.

Mentorship is so important. Outside of what Mr. McVey taught me about language and charity, he and Mr. Hacker and Mr. Ford helped me in practical ways. If I wanted to write a letter to the mayor, for instance, I brought a draft to them for their feedback before sending it off. I did this often—took my two pages to the group, and came back with everything I couldn't say helpfully crossed out. *My goodness*, I would think at the sight of all those strikethrough lines. But I dutifully took their feedback in the spirit it was given and rewrote the letter.

I distinctly remember doing that once and coming away with feedback that said, "This sentence is correct. Everything else needs to be rewritten." Only one sentence out of two pages! My first thought was *No, man*. I did not want to rewrite it yet again.

Of course, I did rewrite it. Why would I squander such an opportunity to learn by choosing not to? These men were helping me in the most effective way possible—by not sparing my feelings as they taught me the kind of excellence required in the business world. And, like the board meeting before, I also think they were testing me yet again—not to see if I could meet their standards, but testing my patience and temper so that I could learn how to remain calm in business dealings.

This group also taught me the importance of doing preparatory work before any meetings took place. I learned to plan out what I needed to say beforehand, to hone and rehearse it. And while these great mentors were all about giving me all the advice I wanted, I was like a curious child with what they could teach me. I wanted to know everything. The result was that wherever I would go in a business capacity, the people I met all commented on the same thing. Walking me out of their offices, they said, "You're so friendly and so professional."

Eventually, I was moved into a bigger office space that enabled me to invite potential clients to my office for coffee and meetings; this was important because I was meeting with ambassadors and dignitaries as I made arrangements for an international pageant. The surroundings my mentors provided me with were critical in building trust with the kind of people I was seeking sponsorship from. And before long, people were contacting me. "I'd like to sponsor two tickets for the pageant winners," I heard. "Do you have enough money for all the food?"

At first, I was shy about asking for the money I needed. I feared that people would think I was cheap or too lazy to do the work myself. But eventually I learned that wasn't the case. Requests for funding are simply a process in the corporate world—one I could learn and then navigate with a fair amount of skill, thanks to my mentors.

And I quickly developed an approach that I still believe in today. Instead of asking for money, I ask to be connected with people who might share my vision and could help me realize it. I don't hide the fact that money is needed. In fact, I always say I need money. I always say, "This is what we have to do," and lay out the needs of the project at hand. But I also always assure whomever I'm speaking with that when it comes to that money, things will work out.

Because they always do.

BUT I WANTED MORE

As I continued to learn so much about Western-style professionalism and business, I quickly developed from a youth into an adult. That's how I think about it. When I started out, I was a boy; on the other side of that project, I had grown into a professional and a man.

I still remember that my girlfriend at the time didn't care for my shift to adult behavior. She dumped me because of it, insisting that if I wanted to be a successful businessperson, we couldn't have a relationship. I understood. It would have been unfair of me to commit to having a family when in my heart, I knew my dreams, ambitions, and goals came first.

I was unusual in that regard. Where I grew up in Africa, when you are young and in a village with a population of about twenty-five, people don't believe that your dreams can come true. And that's not because of a lack of imagination; there are very practical reasons. First and foremost, the poverty in villages like mine is astounding. Second, these parts of Africa lack the infrastructure to propel their youth to dream levels of success. Third, there are fewer opportunities to find success. And perhaps even heavier for each of us is the fourth reason: we are running against time.

Here is what I mean by that. There you are, speaking of your dreams and your parents need food. *Your family needs food.* That's why I got a job selling fruit when I was seven years old. That scenario is true for most people who come from villages like mine. It was true for the girlfriend who dumped me. True to her own heart at the time, she married young and eventually became a teacher. But I've heard from members of my own family that she sometimes wonders whether she could've waited and done other things first.

For my part, I got that job selling fruit to provide bread for my family, but I wanted *more.*

I never stopped talking about my dreams, even when my mom started to ask me whether they could ever really come true. In her mind, I think she thought my dream was simply to become rich and do all the things that rich people do. But the longer I stuck with my dreams, the more I resonated with the white-collar world.

Giving up my girlfriend—not to mention girls in general—was only the first sacrifice I made for my dreams. Distance grew between my friends and me, and I needed to allow that to happen. I couldn't spend my nights drinking with them at the nightclubs in Harare. I simply didn't have the time. My world looked like receiving a letter on Friday that I needed to present to Mr. McVey or another of my mentors on Monday.

So at a certain point, it was time to do only my things. In some ways it was a lonely period in my life, but I could see that if I continued to work at it, I could really reach someone and make a difference, just like Mr. McVey said I should. And that was what I wanted most of all.

After successfully producing the Miss Southern Africa pageant, the mayor of the city of Harare, engineer Elias Mudzuri, presented me with a certificate of appreciation for bringing together so many different countries. It was a joyous moment, one that he also invited the business and diplomatic communities of Harare to witness.

A gentleman from the American Embassy of Public Affairs, Mr. Stephen Mushonga, suggested I try different programs or even go to school. But I thought going to school meant I would have to put aside my dreams and wait. Hadn't I refused my parents' request that I go to college for exactly that reason? Still, I took his suggestion to heart and considered it seriously. Perhaps there was value in going to college.

Meanwhile, I received an email from a woman located in Washington, DC. She'd seen the pageant I organized online—the internet was a relatively new experience for Africa in 2003, but it was starting to come to us—and invited me to Washington to appear as a guest of honor at an international fashion show. The show organizers would even sponsor my hotel and travel expenses while I was in America. I recognized this as a great opportunity.

Slowly and steadily, things were beginning to unfold.

CHAPTER 5
Coming to America

T here was one main hurdle I needed to get past before I could act on the invitation to visit America: I needed a visa.

I still had a valid passport and the European travel visas from my tour, but an American visa was an entirely different matter. At that time, it wasn't yet possible to apply for a visa online. I knew I needed to go in person to the American Embassy to fill in the necessary forms by hand. After submitting them, I would be given an interview date. And I knew that interview was a make-or-break moment.

On the morning of my appointment, I got ready, paying careful attention to my appearance. I shaved and dressed in a black suit and white collared shirt. I'd told my mentors about the interview and opportunity, and true to their supportive natures, Mr. Ford, Mr. Hacker, and Mr. McVey drove me to the embassy and waited for me to finish. It was a touching gesture. Privately, however, I remember thinking to myself that the pressure was on. *My goodness*, I couldn't help but think. *If I'm denied a visa, it will be such an embarrassment.*

I steeled myself and walked inside the embassy. Right away, I noticed I was the youngest person in the room. At that point in my life, being the youngest had become something like my "normal," but on that day I was still shocked. I took my seat, and I looked over at a man, obviously a scholar, wearing his master's robes. He went to the window; I overheard him telling the consular officer conducting his interview that he wanted to continue his research in America.

He was denied.

This will never work, I thought. *If that man got denied, I will, too.*

I continued to observe as the ten people ahead of me were called forward, approached that window, and spoke to the woman conducting interviews. Every single one of them were denied the visa they sought. Can you imagine? There I was, only twenty-five years old, witnessing so many older, more educated individuals be turned away, one after the other after the other.

I began to sweat. Finally, I was called to the window. "What do you do?" the woman on the other side asked.

"I'm a producer."

"Have you done any projects?"

"Yes," I answered. "I produced the Miss Southern Africa pageant."

She looked at me then—really looked. "Can you stand over there for a moment and then walk towards me?" she asked.

I crossed the room, paused, and walked back to the window.

"Yes," she said. "I *do* recognize you. You're that guy who put that pageant together. I saw you there."

Another man came to stand next to me at the window. "Are you organizing Miss Africa International in America?" he asked. "The mayor's office gave us tickets to Miss Southern Africa. We saw you when we came to the event."

What providence! From that point on, these two made everything easy for me. The man asked about why I wanted to go to America, and I showed him a printout of the email I'd received—my invitation to Washington, DC.

"Do you have a bank statement?" the man asked.

I produced my bank statement that showed the sum I had left over after paying all the bills for Miss Southern Africa. The sum was not enough to fund another event, but it was something.

The woman frowned slightly. "Will you get more money from your sponsors?" she asked.

"If I approach them, yes," I said, fully confident in that truth. "They will give."

She considered that for a moment. "If you go to America, how do I know that you don't plan on running away and staying there? How do I know you'll come back?"

There it was. The most important question of all. I knew that my American dream depended on my answer.

"I ran a very popular event in Africa," I began, "one that you attended and witnessed. You've seen what I do, but take a look at these."

I handed her a book I'd brought with me. It was stuffed full of press releases about me and the projects I'd been part of. She began leafing through the pages, and I saw her comparing names with all the other paperwork I'd brought along. Although she recognized me from the event, she still needed to prove that I was actually Ashley Shumba and not someone pretending to be me so that they could leave the country and disappear in America.

Finally, she looked up at her colleague. "Yes, it's him," she said, before turning her gaze on me. "You don't have a wife or children?"

I understood what she was getting at. Having ties to Africa like a wife and children would mean I was more likely to come back when my visa ended. But I did not have those particular ties to my home continent.

I shook my head. "If you feel like I don't qualify to go to America, I can only travel to countries that have admitted me, like France and England. I'll produce my events there."

She paused. A thousand emotions flew through me at that moment. My mouth went dry. Finally, she handed my paperwork back to me but kept my passport for processing.

"Come back on Wednesday and collect your passport and visa, Ashley," she said. "You're going to America. Safe travels!"

I did my best to thank her and maintain professionalism as I exited the building. But as soon as I got outside, I took off running toward the car where my mentors waited.

"You're going to America!" they said.

Indeed, I was.

FINALLY, AMERICA

Before I left Africa, I met with the director of the Zambian Embassy. He happened to be a friend of mine and had heard I was traveling to America as an honored guest. He told me he wanted to contribute to my trip by paying for my ticket and providing me with some pocket money. He was genuinely excited for me to go, as was my uncle Biriam, who gave me money for the trip as well. Thus fortified, I boarded a plane.

What was I feeling at that moment? There I was, on the cusp of attaining the dream I'd cherished in my heart for so long. I was overwhelmed; I was anxious. I knew that what had started as a dream was about to become my reality, and I could already see myself in movies. Holding that picture in my mind, I relaxed and settled in for the long flight.

After a brief stopover in New York, I arrived in Washington DC in 2003 for the next Miss Africa International Pageant. I attended the event that showcased the rich heritage of over thirty different African countries to an American audience of diplomats and celebrities. I was seated in the front row and introduced to that well-appointed audience as a distinguished guest from Africa. I was pleased that everything went so well.

Unfortunately, however, whatever professional opportunity I had hoped to find in DC died out after the event. I continued to seek avenues and sponsors that would help me fund other projects, but to no avail. The contacts I'd hoped to make never materialized. Though it pained me, I had to admit that I was struggling. The experience was far from the American Dream I'd imagined.

However, I had gotten a call from a colleague of mine, Rodney Manzanga, who lived in Philadelphia. Rodney was close to my age and was a student at the University of Philadelphia. "Come to Philly," he said, after listening to me describe my struggles. "Let's see what we can do."

Perhaps Rodney's invitation was an open door into a better experience than I was having, I thought. Perhaps Washington DC just wasn't the right place for the project I imagined, but perhaps Philadelphia could be. I packed my bags, bought a bus ticket, and steeled myself with resolve. No matter the obstacle, I would always continue to try. I would keep moving forward.

That is who I am, I reminded myself. *I will always believe the best and keep my focus.*

I arrived in Philadelphia and stayed with Rodney for the next couple of months, doing what I could to contribute to the household, such as buying food and other necessities. We were young and at times liked to have fun, going clubbing and taking trips out of state to Connecticut and North Carolina with our hired car.

It all felt a bit silly to me, but for the first time in my life, I was having fun connecting with people I thought of as my age mates. Building friendships with other men my age felt right to me at the time. And even I can admit that I enjoyed those nights of partying. After a lifetime of hustling, grinding, and relentless focus, it was nice not to worry about life or push toward what I needed to do next.

I allowed my focus to drift for a while. But after a couple of months of doing nothing, I reached a breaking point. I realized that I was tired of being idle. In Africa I had been famous and productive, but when I looked at my life in America, I saw it taking a nosedive instead of moving forward.

Suddenly it seemed to me that the things I had been doing in Africa were more productive and meaningful than anything I had done in America. I felt stuck there in Philadelphia. Stagnant. And I began to realize an uncomfortable truth. Despite all the hope and eagerness and certainty I'd felt about this fabled "Land of Opportunity," America had not helped me further my dreams and goals. If anything, it had distanced me from them.

No, I thought. *This is not my life.*

OUT OF TIME

Meanwhile, I was receiving calls from individuals and corporations that had supported me and wanted to ask about my progress. "What happened?" I heard repeatedly from companies who had sponsored my efforts. In the same breath, many of them also offered me lucrative sponsorship packages to come back to Africa and continue my work there. It felt wonderful to have those assurances and know that if I went back home, I wouldn't be stuck like I had become in America. I would be self-employed. Independent. Successful.

And on top of the phone calls, my visa was ending. I knew I had to go back to Africa before violating my immigration status. The law clearly states that a person who remains in the US beyond the period they have been authorized to stay will have their visa canceled and possibly face immigration problems, including deportation or removal proceedings.

But to return home, I needed money for a ticket. I knew I had some funds coming to me eventually, but if I waited that long I would overstay my visa—something my instincts were clearly telling me not to do. My family members and friends did not understand when I told them I needed to come home so soon. To them, a year in America was a very short space of time. But I knew that if I violated my immigration rights by overstaying my visa, it would jeopardize any future trips or business I hoped to make. For my part, I had always known in my heart that I needed to preserve a path back to America for myself, and I was certain that I *wanted* to come back. This trip might not have been fruitful in the ways I'd hoped, but I still believed in America. I still believed in my dream.

So—money.

All right, I thought. *I'm a man. I'm not too young to do something for myself.* I knew I didn't have to wait around, hoping the funds I needed would fall from the sky. I could work and earn on my own. I considered my options. *You always hear about people working in restaurants*, I reasoned. *Why not try it, even just for the fun of it?*

Off I went to a restaurant I knew from my time in Philly and asked if they were hiring. Right away, the manager brought me on as a dishwasher. And, after two days, the owner told me he wanted to train me to work at the till instead. "I see you have some experience," he said. I worked at this restaurant for close to three months, saving each and every penny I could for the return flight to Africa.

But by then I had run out of time on my visa. I accepted the inevitable: it was time for me to return to Zimbabwe.

Things will be better when I return, I reasoned.

But that was not to be the case. Unbeknownst to me, I received an email sometime while I was soaring over the Atlantic Ocean, one that would break my heart and alter the course of my life.

A DESPERATE MOVE

I arrived in Zimbabwe to tragedy. The email I didn't know about told me that my uncle Biriam, who had always supported me as I pursued my dreams, would not be there to collect me from the airport as planned. He and his wife Audrey had been in a horrific car accident and rushed to the hospital.

I did eventually get the email before landing in Zimbabwe, and when we arrived in my home country, I rushed to get off the plane so that I could get to the hospital as soon as possible.

My new transportation from the airport was there. My brother Thulani Cecil had come to pick me up. Thulani Cecil has since passed, but at that time he was a very successful real estate manager who did well for himself and his family. I was glad to see him. As we left the airport, I kept waiting for him to say something about my uncle, but instead he drove me to a restaurant and then to his office. I thought perhaps he wanted me to work for him, but he didn't seem happy. *Maybe because Biriam was involved in an accident*, I thought. Unable to wait for news any longer, I finally said, "Before we go home, can we go to the hospital and see Biriam?"

"No," he said, shock passing over his face. "Ashley, I'm so sorry. He died."

My beloved uncle, the person who had supported me and

believed in me from the very beginning was gone. I couldn't quite believe it. It broke my heart.

Before I learned of Biriam's accident, I had already been planning my next trip back to America. Despite the professional challenges I'd faced there, I knew I had left on a good note. I hadn't violated my immigration privileges, so I was free to reapply for another visit and would likely be readmitted to the country. What better way to honor the man who had always supported my dreams than by recommitting to them? Although I was heartbroken, I began gathering the necessary paperwork.

But then one morning, as I was filling out my application, the phone rang. It was Biriam's widow, my aunt Audrey. She was still in the hospital, recovering from a deep cut on her forehead that she had sustained during the accident that took my uncle's life.

"Ashley," she said, "will you help me take the kids back and forth to school?"

When Biriam died, he'd left behind five children. The youngest was only three months old. Audrey desperately needed help, and I knew I could give it. Plus, despite my best intentions, I had come to realize my heart wasn't really committed to a second trip to America. I was too broken to be committed to anything.

After Audrey's call, I decided to take a gap year to help her and to process my grief for my uncle. To some, perhaps that sounds foolish. But I was young—and in that youth, I was confident that I could step away for a while and then bounce back stronger than before. And, I reasoned, I had proven my character when I complied with immigration laws. That decision alone would help me bounce forward someday.

But that year proved to be more impactful than I anticipated. While I was helping Audrey and moving through my grief, an economic crisis was developing in Zimbabwe. The situation came as a huge blow to almost everyone as the Zimbabwean dollar lost value and crashed with the market. As a result, many businesses and companies closed their doors.

But in 2005, the famous Kiki Divaris contacted me a second time with a different request: to produce the Miss Zimbabwe pageant that would air live on television. I found myself at press conferences sitting beside Kiki, the Greek modeling maven, philanthropist, and creator of the Miss Zimbabwe pageant. She gave a generation of young girls who watched her pageant on television the dream of one day becoming Miss Zimbabwe.

For my part, it felt like a step in the right direction for my career. The fact that the pageant would be televised brought even more publicity for me and the event, and that could only build my reputation as a producer. But as the economic situation in Zimbabwe continued to deteriorate and so many businesses shuttered, funding for the event stagnated. Many of the workers, including me, lost their jobs.

I was in desperate need of a backup plan in an economic environment where widespread job loss was affecting so many. Despite the poverty in parts of Zimbabwe, it had been considered in the years of my youth to be the "breadbasket" of the continent. But like many others, I was now forced to recognize that it was no longer the country I had grown up in. Knowing that, I decided to move.

I packed what little I had along with my passport and took a bus to Namibia, a neighboring country where I knew no one and had zero contacts. It was a journey of two days by road. My family was against the move, and I knew it was high-risk, but I had considered what my future would be if I stayed in Zimbabwe.

It was a future I did not want for myself. So I relied on one of my unique strengths: to always take calculated risks. And I made the move.

PHOTO ALBUM

At the village in Mberengwa, Zimbabwe, 1979. My mum told me I wasn't keen to have my picture taken. This explains why I looked worried.

At age seven in my village in Zimbabwe, 1984. I'm selling beverages on behalf of a neighbor during drought season.

A self-employed man and the youngest ever upcoming entrepreneur to own a production company in Africa, Zimbabwe.

With international renowned superstar Oliver Mtukudzi.

*On a tour of Europe with the Vuka Africa Dance Group,
part of an international youth exchange program,
1999. I am center among those standing.*

*Mr. Ian McVey, my mentor. Ian was born in 1936. He's still alive and
based in England but struggles with health and aging issues. This
picture was taken in 2014 and was the last time I met him in London
on the way to Africa with my wife. I check up on him every month.*

*My late uncle Biriam Wabatagore and his wife Audrey Wabatagore.
These mentors played a very important role in my life.*

*In 2002, at age twenty-five, I was honored by the mayor
of the city of Harare for having successfully produced
the Miss Southern Africa Pageant. At that time I was the
youngest entrepreneur and producer in Africa.*

In 1999 in Britain with the Mayor of London. This is a group of multi-talented young people drawn from Africa to participate on an international youth exchange program.

My dad as best man at Mr. Paul Stevens's wedding. In 1984 Mr. Stevens took the picture that is on this book's front cover.

In 2003 I arrived in the United States after being invited to attend an international event in Washington, DC as a guest of honor from Africa.

At a press conference after being hired as a producer by the Miss Zimbabwe Trust, Zimbabwe, 2016. I am surrounded by beauty queens, and to my far left is the late Mrs. Kiki Divaris, the patron and chairperson.

With my siblings Thulani and Thelma, 1980. The tall lady is one of our relatives who visited us at our village homestead.

My first time ever eating lunch at an upmarket restaurant, Harare, 1996.

*With my parents and close family members at
my late brother Thulani's wedding.*

*I was honored by the Ambassador of Zimbabwe for providing
formal and informal employment to both the Namibian
and Zimbabwean communities, Namibia, 2012.*

*With less privileged children after making a
sound donation, Namibia, 2012.*

*With Bilaal Ameen, England, 2012. Bilaal is the British
gentlemen I accidentally met in the streets of Zimbabwe who
selected me to go to Europe for his youth exchange program.*

With Rosalinde Nakale and Klaudia Kay, Namibia, 2012. Rosalinde and Klaudia were very successful businesswomen in Namibia at the time. We did many construction and philanthropy projects together.

In 2012 I arrived at Universal Studios in Hollywood for auditions. I was straight from Africa, with less than a week in the US, and was already trying to have a breakthrough in American showbiz.

*As a bus/truck driver, Philadelphia, 2013. This is when
I learned about the transport business and became
motivated to register my own trucking company.*

*At Philadelphia Airport Terminal A. Behind me is the couch that
once served as my bed when I briefly became homeless in 2013.*

I was briefly a limousine driver. I deliberately joined the limo career to network and meet celebrities and business executives with the hope for future collaborations and business partnerships. It worked out well for me.

With my wife at our wedding ceremony, 2013. To show Marie my love and gratitude, I bought her the dress for five thousand dollars. She kept the dress to one day gift it to our daughter on her wedding day.

*With our bridal party, West Chester, Pennsylvania,
2013. A very special day and moment.*

*With Marie on our honeymoon, Britain, 2014. Afterward, we traveled
to Zimbabwe to introduce her to my parents and relatives.*

With my late dad, New York City, 2017. This was his first time to be in the US or on an international trip. He was seventy-seven in this photo.

With my business associate who is based in Africa. Ms. Maphano is an emerging young entrepreneur who owns a beauty salon and spa in the Kingdom of Lesotho.

At a collaboration with Avani Hotels to host the next annual Global Small Business Awards ceremony, Lesotho, 2019.

I was a guest of honor at the Miss High School Zimbabwe pageant, Harare, 2020. The winner would proceed to take part in the Miss High School Africa pageant, an event I founded, produced, and own.

At our homestead during the COVID-19 lockdown, Mberengwa, Zimbabwe, 2020. Saving the villagers with balanced hot meals.

With my mum in the village, 2024. She is eighty years old.
Since the passing of my dad, I travel to Zimbabwe every
year to spend time with her and glean more wisdom.

*My first time meeting Brian Dawkins after a
fruitful limo ride, Philadelphia, 2022.*

*With Audrey Wabatagore, the wife of my late uncle Biriam
Wabatagore, at her daughter's wedding, England, 2023. This
woman is my hero, and I can't thank her enough for believing in
my dreams and taking me into her home when I was a teenager.*

Following an Eagles game, Brian Dawkins introduced me to his lovely wife Connie, Philadelphia, 2023.

With my book project partners Brian Dawkins (NFL Hall of Fame) and John Glomb (President and CEO of Philadelphia Insurance Companies), 2024. These two fine gentlemen made it possible for my book to be published.

With Edward Gall and his wife Lesley, my family friends and real estate mentors.

With Brian Dawkins as distinguished guests at the Union League of Philadelphia ceremony, 2024.

CHAPTER 6
Building Back in Namibia

F inding opportunity and employment in Namibia turned out to be more difficult than I could possibly have imagined. I spent four months looking for a job while attempting to start creative projects. I got nowhere, and I exhausted my savings in the process.

At long last, I was hired on as a builder and assistant by a large Chinese construction company. The salary they offered me—if it could even be called a salary—was a pittance. Such a small salary made me feel used and taken advantage of, but I had no choice but to accept the job and do the best with it that I could.

But I would soon learn that the words "builder" and "assistant" in my job description were nothing more than euphemisms for hard labor. The job I had accepted was truly modern-day slavery.

Once again, I was heartbroken—but for a completely different reason this time. I couldn't stop thinking of my background in theater and production, or of my time with an office in my mentors' building, or of my travels around Europe and America. How could those things have led to these circumstances? How could I have ended up like this?

I told no one at the construction job about my past. I felt that if any of my coworkers found out, they would see how far I had fallen, and I would be left with nothing but shame. It was simply too embarrassing. So instead of talking about my dreams and what I had done, I worked hard. Even if I had nothing else, I still had my character, and that meant something to me.

But I often looked at my surroundings, at the squalor brought about by such difficult working conditions, and wondered at my existence. I'd left my home country to escape the ills of poverty and strife, hadn't I? And yet, it seemed I had "escaped" right into the lowest point of my life.

MODERN-DAY SLAVERY

After three months of hard labor, my supervisor took notice of my honest character and promoted me to be the door man at the company's warehouse. He informed me that I would be responsible for controlling the inventory; this meant I would be counting all incoming and outgoing material. I readily agreed. Surely a promotion was a step in the right direction, wasn't it?

But then, early one Saturday morning, a woman showed up at the warehouse. I recognized her as part of the family who owned the company. In fact, she was the owner's sister. Perhaps that family connection explains why she thought I would allow her to smuggle 300 bricks and three ton bags of cement out of the warehouse, unaccounted for.

She was mistaken.

It was a security guard who tipped me off to the situation. "Ash," he said, "I need you to sign for this."

I looked at the paper he held in front of me. There was no receipt, no invoice, and no quote—only an order for what amounted to close to a thousand US dollars in supplies and equipment. "Who is this for?" I asked. "This is a lot of equipment to move from the company without being reported. I cannot authorize this; it needs a signature from the owner."

The security guard informed her of my refusal, and she approached me, intent on having her way. I stood my ground, making it clear that I would not allow her to move that much company property without authorization. For all I knew, she was doing everything in secret and planning to sell it somewhere. "You won't steal those bricks and cement bags," I said.

My refusal angered her. She immediately went to her brother with a fabricated story, claiming that I disrespected her and that I was trying to divide their family.

A short time later, the company owner came to me. "Can I see you in my office?" he asked.

I followed him to his office and calmly explained everything that had happened. "Am I allowed to do this for her?" I asked. "If I am, then anyone can walk in here, pay nothing, and take whatever they want."

He got up, went around his desk, and closed the office door. "Ash," he said, "you are a young person, and what you did is remarkable. You did exactly what you are supposed to do. I don't know what my sister is doing or why she did that. It isn't allowed.

"But now, the situation in my family is so bad that I don't think it will be easy for you to work here. This is a family business, and this thing is weighing heavily on my family. So here's what I'm going to do. I will pay you for the next couple of months while you look for another job. You're not being fired or leaving because you did anything wrong. It's only to keep the peace within my family and our business."

I considered his offer. The situation was unfair, but his offer was generous and kind. Still, I wanted a record that it was my honesty that cost me my job, nothing more.

"Okay," I said, "I will leave. But I want you to write me a reference letter stating what you just told me—that I chose the right course of action, and I'm not leaving because I did anything wrong."

He enthusiastically agreed and promised to write for me.

By the next morning, almost two hundred employees had heard that I wasn't coming back to work anymore. They had learned the whole truth of the situation, and many of them harbored no love for the sister who had caused me to leave.

If I had been someone else, my leaving might have created a bit of company gossip and nothing more. But over the months of my employment, I had grown close with the owner and taken it upon myself to be an advocate for all the people employed at his company. I kept them abreast of personnel changes that could impact them and vouchered their lunch allowances. My leaving meant they were now on their own.

As a united voice, these wonderful people approached their supervisor to ask where I was. "If Ashley is not here," they said, "we're not coming to work either." They went on strike, and before long, the incident was all over the news.

Seeing hundreds of people lay down their tools for my sake left me in awe. I felt such love, such belonging, and it was truly an extraordinary moment. But the strike also caught the attention of a particular person who worked high in the Namibian government, and she was about to pick up the phone. To call *me*.

LOOKING UP

Losing a job, for whatever reason, is incredibly stressful. I was grateful for the severance pay I received from the construction company owner, but my bills and expenses were still piling up.

And then one day, my phone rang. I answered and heard a woman on the other end of the line. She explained who she was and told me that she worked in government. I would later learn that she also privately owned multiple properties and was actively working on projects in connection with them. "I've seen all the news coverage of your story," she said, "and I think you're a very good person. I want you to come and work for me."

I was stunned. "Work for you?" I repeated.

"Yes, but you can't just work for me. Based on what you did at that construction company, and the actions your coworkers took when you weren't allowed back, I can tell that you're more than just a 'worker.' I'd like to offer you a contract."

A contract? Again, I was stunned—this time, into silence.

"Number one," she continued, "people obviously trust your leadership. Number two, even the company confirmed that you did nothing wrong and were forced out because of a family dispute. You're worthy of a contract because you are a leader, and based on what I've seen, you're a leader I can trust."

It never ceases to amaze me how things can turn around. That morning, I'd had no prospects, no opportunities—nothing but bills and uncertainty. And within hours, I'd been offered a lucrative contract from someone I'd never even met. It was more than I could have hoped for.

After that, I couldn't help but think my high-risk move to Namibia had paid off handsomely. Certainly the move itself played a role in my ability to keep pursuing my dreams. But when I really think about it, more credit is due to the fact that I made sure I always acted honestly and with integrity.

It would've been far easier to just let that woman steal those bricks and cement bags. I could go back even farther and say it would've been even simpler to have just stayed in America with an expired visa. But in my life, I have always understood that there is depthless value in honest words and actions. As I hung up the phone, I couldn't help thinking that sometimes, that value *also* shows up in dollar amounts.

Under the contract I was offered that day, I worked as a site manager and eventually a contractor from 2007 to 2012. Those were five years that changed my life—and the lives of so many others in Namibia.

BUILDING DREAMS

As I've written, the economy in Africa experiences seasons of extraordinary difficulty. As a result, people often multitask between different industries to be able to provide for their families. It was one such economic crisis that had pushed me out of Zimbabwe and into Namibia in the first place, into an industry I'd never intended to enter.

And while I hadn't experienced immediate success in the construction business, my circumstances changed considerably with the contract I landed. I was able to rediscover construction as an industry vital to creating spaces that connect communities and provide jobs that enrich society itself.

By 2011, I had experienced considerable personal financial success. I partnered with two prominent women in Namibia, Rosalinde Nakale and Klaudia Kay, in executing a charity organization called Heal Southern Africa Foundation that would cater to less privileged children. Rosalinde and Klaudia believed so much in my leadership and creative skills that they asked me to take on the role of project director.

As these women and I became more involved in additional profit and nonprofit projects together, I discovered an added benefit: we were creating both informal and formal employment. And, in a break with tradition, these jobs were available to both men and women.

In the years leading up to 2011, many communities in Africa deprived women of the same opportunities to work that men enjoyed. (This was especially true in the construction industry, which had been traditionally dominated by men.) But in recent years, that attitude was changing. My continent was demonstrating its commitment to promote gender equality and the empowerment of women.

For my part, I was thrilled to witness the rise of two women who were determined to make their mark in such a male-dominated industry. I was also proud to partner with them. They both came from a poverty-stricken neighborhood, and they were on a mission to empower more women to step into professional spaces and have careers.

That fits with my personal ethos. I believe women should be given the same opportunities as men to earn a living in whatever way they choose. We need women at all levels of business, including—and perhaps especially—at the top. To help advance these efforts, my partners and I included language on our job postings that encouraged women to apply. We held a vision of women at all levels of industry, including at the top, as our north star throughout the course of the project.

That's not to say we were running a large corporation—we were not, and we didn't employ very many people. But the little we did was still a lot compared with other businesses in the area, and we gained recognition and support from other organizations that existed to empower women from the surrounding community.

About a year later, in 2012, I was honored to receive an excellence award from the ambassador of the Embassy of Zimbabwe in Namibia in acknowledgement of my tireless efforts and immeasurable support to the Zimbabwean community of Namibia through job creation. When the ambassador called me to her office, I once again discovered the fruits of maintaining my personal integrity and character. "I want to recognize what you are doing," she said. "You have an outstanding character, and I appreciate what you are doing for Zimbabwean immigrants here."

For me, being recognized by such a high-profile government official was an extraordinary moment—one that was deeply meaningful to me. I often mused on my change in circumstances in Namibia, and I knew that if I stayed in that country, I could become even more successful. And in my years there, I had made wonderful friends that would have made my staying even better. Those friends, whom I'd met through my career and who had worked alongside me on many projects, had become a second family to me—my home away from home.

But for all that, I could also see that the Namibian government's involvement in businesses was having an adverse effect on the economy that would likely only get worse. In the back of my mind, the logic that had driven me from Zimbabwe began to simmer again—as did my American dream.

Meanwhile, I continued to find success in the construction industry. Much of my income went to pay my employees and to purchase and maintain the necessary equipment. But what was left out of that amount was still a considerable sum, all things considered, and so I followed the advice of my old mentor Mr. McVey and remembered those in my community who were less fortunate than me. I had never forgotten his words about helping others in need, and I kept room for charity in my heart.

Every day I witnessed the sheer number of "street kids" in the city of Windhoek, Namibia—kids who weren't able to pay school fees and therefore did not attend school. Remembering what education had done for me, a person from such humble beginnings, I resolved to do what I could to help these children. I started a small foundation with the funds that were left over from my earnings and went to the press. "I'm looking for a hundred kids who have problems paying their school fees," I said.

And suddenly, things began to happen.

First, I was able to execute my vision to pay school fees for less privileged children, and I will always be grateful for the opportunity to do so. To see their smiling faces was an incredible reward. But then, after speaking to the press, I received an astonishing offer from the Department of Information and Communication Technology. They asked if I would like to work for the Namibia Broadcasting Corporation as a spokesperson for the network. It was a tempting offer, and it wasn't lost on me that I would be many steps closer to the arts industry if I accepted. And yet, I turned it down. By that time my sights were firmly set on returning to the USA.

At the time, I was heartened by the reason all these amazing invitations were reaching me. Each one was, in its way, a recognition of what I had done for others and a recognition of the fact that I was able to accomplish remarkable things.

"How is he doing more for Namibia than its own people?" I often heard from government officials and businesspeople. "He's more trusted and lives better than us, too—perhaps even better than a US citizen!"

To say I surprised people is an understatement. There I was, a young person, a person of color, and an immigrant to Namibia, and I was funding children's school fees while running a construction company that was so busy and successful, I had hired out all the construction equipment and machinery available for a solid month. At that point in my construction career, banks were even calling me to ask if I needed another loan—not the other way around.

My success in business was the reason I received a call from the secretary of the former president of Namibia. The secretary had heard of me; he asked me to his office because he wanted to learn my secret to success. How was I running such a prolific business? How had I become so successful that my business had built apartment buildings large enough to accommodate almost fifty families?

He also wanted to learn more about my interest in humanitarianism. I told him how charity work is often viewed as the backbone of a community. It helps sustain communities and has the added benefit of reducing stress and boosting personal happiness in the giver. For me personally, knowing that I can still make a difference in a world filled with uncertainties and chaos is a balm to the soul. Often in my life, charity work has also been the secret to living a life that is not only happier, but healthier, wealthier, more productive, and more meaningful.

I also acknowledged that having the power to improve others' lives is a privilege—one that comes with a sense of obligation. Unfortunately, governments and societies are not always set up to protect everyone who needs protecting. That's the simple reality. It's also why charities and charity work are so important—both can fill the gap in provision for those who need it most. Helping can also grow belonging, and belonging can grow connections.

That is not to say we should help others with the intent of getting something out of it. No. We should help for the sake of helping, to improve the welfare of another, without expectations. But that doesn't change what *can* happen when we choose to help.

During my years as a contractor in Namibia, I often took walks with my friends on the weekends as a way to refresh after the hustle of the workweek. We usually did our weekly shopping in the market, but we also just hung out. The point was to spend time relaxing together.

It was on one such Saturday, while walking through the streets, that my friends and I came upon a gentleman who had stopped his pickup truck (in Namibia, they're called *bakkies*) along the side of the road. As we walked closer, he approached us, introduced himself as Mr. Riaan Mouton, and asked if we knew anyone who needed work. He was looking for someone to paint the exterior of his house.

He had directed his questions to me, but we decided as a group to take the job ourselves. Since it was a weekend, we went back to his house with him right there on the spot. The job turned out to be an easy one, and by Sunday, we were finished. That job led to another, larger painting project with Mr. Mouton, this one an extensive commercial property that housed his cell phone repair business.

My friends and I were shocked by the scope of the project. "Remember, we're not professional painters," we said. "We only took the job to paint your house as a weekend project away from our regular jobs."

But Mr. Mouton insisted, and we eventually agreed. We knew we had to work smart to pull it off, so we hired a few people who had the painting knowledge and expertise we lacked. The job took three weeks, but our strategy paid off. Mr. Mouton paid us handsomely for a job well done.

What began as a working relationship with Mr. Mouton and his wife, Yolande, developed into a friendship. They encouraged me as I developed my professional construction career in Namibia. After a few years, they decided to leave the city, and by that time I owned my construction business. Mr. Mouton and his wife insisted on investing in me and my business to help it grow. Ever the entrepreneur, I used those funds to instead open a grocery shop, which I eventually sold to a friend.

Because America was calling again.

HELLO KISMET, MY OLD FRIEND

One day while I was sitting in my office, I happened to look out the window and see a gentleman pushing his car down the road. He was alone. *What a heavy burden for one person*, I thought. My instincts told me to help, so that is precisely what I did.

It wasn't until we were shoulder to shoulder, pushing his car down the road, that I learned he was an American diplomat. We talked while we pushed, discussing many issues along the way. Afterwards, he invited me to his office to continue the conversation, and I agreed.

My only intent had been to help someone who seemed to need it, but the moment changed my life. Meeting a high-profile diplomat was a moment of kismet, similar to the one I'd experienced all those years ago when I escorted Bilaal through the streets of Harare. Here was someone I could ask about how the procedures moved and what I needed to do to return to America.

Within weeks I began the process of applying for a new visa. I was no stranger to the scary side of that process—the seemingly unending sixty-day waiting period, countless appointments and interviews, and the possibility of a rejection letter at the end. That's what many people experienced, I knew, although my first process had been helped along. Thankfully, this time around, my new diplomatic friend helped make the process easy. My visa was approved, and I began wrapping up all my existing projects to prepare for this new journey of a lifetime.

Normally, when a country gives someone a visa, they are very specific about it. Based on my accomplishments in Namibia, the visa office saw me first and foremost as a businessperson traveling to the United States to make contacts and potentially establish a company. They awarded me a business visa for those purposes.

Upon being granted a visa I called my mentor Rosalinde Nakale and told her the good news—I was going to America. She was overwhelmed with joy for me. "When are you traveling," she asked, "and do you have an air ticket?"

"I am leaving as soon as possible but do not have my air ticket yet."

"In acknowledgement of your tireless efforts and outstanding character in Namibia," she responded, "I will afford you a free air ticket to New York. Please allow this gesture as a gift for being an exemplary young man to our youth. May God bless you and make a way for you in America."

Now it was my turn to be overwhelmed at her generosity, kindness, and provision. I thanked her profusely and considered my destination.

Where am I going to go? I wondered. New York and Chicago seemed like viable options. But before I left, I called my old friend Bilal Ameen, who I had escorted through the streets of Harare and who had chosen me for the European tour all those years before. We hadn't stayed in constant contact over the last ten-plus years, so I googled him and found his email address.

"I'll be passing through London on my way to New York," I wrote. "I would love to get together if you're available."

Bilal readily agreed. "Your timing is wonderful," he said. He told me his son, an established actor in Hollywood in his own right, was working on a documentary film about the Youth Exchange Program that had taken me to Europe so many years before. "I'm doing the documentary with him, and I would love for you to be a part of it."

I quickly applied for a British visa that was granted again. Despite the fact that both of these processes in Africa can be quite difficult, I'd managed to accomplish everything in a short amount of time.

In those days, I often thought that God worked in amazing ways. I could hardly believe so many opportunities were coming to me at once. But in my experience, that has happened time and again. Once a single door opens, others start to open as well.

One such door opened while I was preparing for my move to America. I received a call from the director of the United States Agency for International Development, who wanted to discuss the best ways to develop Namibia through youth empowerment and assistance. I attended that meeting, which was primarily focused on young people who were in business with Klaudia Kay. A study had been commissioned and interviews with the youths in question, asking what assistance they would find the most helpful, had been undertaken. We were resolutely against giving the wrong type of service to the young people in Namibia.

It was wonderful to see these young people respond. In effect, their responses showed us where the gap in assistance was, allowing us to do what was needed to close it. A wide range of programs were suggested, including teaching female students to make clothing for the fashion and design industry—an industry that our young people saw was always growing and changing—so that they could evolve along with it. Other industries that could improve the lives and working conditions of these youth were also proposed, as were ways to provide funding, amounts needed, and criteria for choosing recipients.

All in all, the meeting was an eye opener for me. Despite my own humble beginnings, I learned about challenges I had not personally faced. I was able to know and understand these challenges through the words of the young people who had faced them by reading and listening to the interviews that had been conducted as part of the survey process. Through the meeting, I got connected with several of these young people—people who possessed great talent and only needed to be connected with others through the right channels and showcase their talents.

That was something I understood to my core. In many ways, it has been the whole of my adult life.

PEARLS

It wasn't lost on me that I was stopping over in London to offer my voice and story for a film project. My friends and I had always joked around about my rise and how it would lead to my eventual return to America, but we never thought the day would come so soon.

When the time came, I bid them a very emotional goodbye, knowing in my heart that if things worked out for me in America the way I hoped they would, I might never see them again. Distance can wreak havoc on relationships; would our friendships survive the thousands of miles, the ocean, and the many time zones I was about to put between myself and Namibia?

Of course, there was no way of knowing. So while that goodbye was incredibly hard, I recognized it for what it was: the beginning of something new for me. I accepted the intervention of fate in my life, held my friends in a special place in my heart, and got on an airplane, the familiar words my friends and I had often repeated to each other echoing in my mind.

The world is our oyster.

CHAPTER 7
America, Again

When I arrived at Heathrow Airport in London, Bilal was there waiting for me. Over ten years had passed since we'd last seen each other. We had both been so young back then; now the years were showing on both of us. But our hearts, I think, were still the same. We caught up on a decade's worth of news, and I told him I was going back to America to pursue my Hollywood dream. We went to his filming location and shot my part in the documentary alongside many of the other participants

Through his documentary, I would have the opportunity to share my story with the British audience. In my heart, I felt overwhelming gratitude for a people who would support youths from outside their country and give them the chance to see more. "Thank you for putting up a program for the youths," I said when the camera began rolling. "It is one of the most inspiring things for someone at a tender age to grow up knowing that we live for more than ourselves."

Because truly, that is what Bilal's program had done for me— opened my eyes to *more* and strengthened my desire to bring that awareness to other youths in my country. I am eternally grateful for that opportunity. Later, Bilaal introduced me to his children and his wife in their new home.

When it was time for me to depart for New York, Bilal did something wonderful. He handed me a sheet of paper, on which he'd written the names and contact information for individuals he knew in Hollywood. It was a wealth of names: people involved in the movie *Black Panther*; Ziggy Marley, Bob Marley's son; Bilal's son, Aml; and others. It was as if he'd just handed me a key to the American movie and music industry. Holding that paper, I felt the old dreams stirring in me with renewed strength.

I made very few practical arrangements, like accommodations, before I left, but that mattered little. My faith in God had grown into a faith without borders. I had begun to believe that he would allow me to step into the greater unknown. I believed in his will for my life, his goodness, his purpose, and his promises. I entrusted him with my life.

I clearly remembered how things had gone for me in America the last time, and so I knew I was taking a crazy risk. But at the same time, something supernatural was pushing me forward to pursue the American Dream. I believed then what I believe now: that "supernatural something" was God's hand on my life, drawing me out into the unknown. I grasped that hand and stepped out in faith. I still didn't know what my path would look like when I got to America, but whatever it looked like, I knew I was ready to walk it.

DREAM CHASER

My flight from London ended in New York. When I arrived, I found myself in Grand Central Station with one overwhelming thought. *No. I can't be in New York.*

There were so many people, so much traffic, and such a busy lifestyle throbbing all around me that I knew it wasn't the place for me. With that certainty, I purchased a train ticket and settled in for the long ride to Chicago. Can you imagine? There I was, alone and carrying all my worldly possessions in a few suitcases, not knowing where I was going. And when I arrived in Chicago, I felt the same as I had in New York.

I cannot be here, either, I thought. Like New York, Chicago was too chaotic. And if I was being honest with myself, I knew my heart was still in Hollywood.

My American dream was growing bigger and bigger in my heart. Since Bilal had handed me that paper in London, I'd felt the tug to join the ranks of producers and artists in Hollywood growing stronger. Perhaps it was instinct, urging me ever westward. *Hollywood is where dreams come true,* I reasoned. Why go anywhere else?

So I boarded another train. For the next two days, I watched the lands and cities of America fly past my window as I wondered what I would do when I arrived in Hollywood. Like many in this country who have made a similar pilgrimage, I felt excited and nervous. Idea after idea passed through my thoughts and a million scenarios played out in my imagination. Which would be true? Any of them? None of them?

When I arrived in Hollywood, I unloaded my bags and carried them off the train. The feeling of arrival was overwhelming. *I am finally here,* I thought. *I made it.*

Right away, I began visiting famous landmarks, taking pictures of myself in front of them. As I did, the scores of homeless individuals baffled me. There was so much talent in Hollywood. Why were so many sleeping on the streets there? But I comforted myself with a single reassurance: *They are them and I'm me.* In other words, their path was not the one I was walking.

I continued taking pictures and posting them for my family and friends. To them, I was a superstar—and, truthfully, I saw myself that way, too. I felt in my bones that I was already famous and successful. Soon, I too would be one of the celebrities being mobbed by paparazzi and adoring fans. All I had to do was step into my first film and make my breakthrough official.

I began looking for that treasured piece of paper from Bilal, so that I could begin my calls. I searched my pockets. I searched my bags. Fear crept in as my search grew frantic.

The paper was . . . gone. How could it be gone? How could I have lost something so important, so precious?

What am I going to do now? I thought.

My first instinct was to secure lodging. Unfortunately, LA prices were such that a hotel room would cost me around $300 a night—a cost that would quickly drain my funds. I continued walking around, getting my bearings and learning my options. Eventually I stumbled upon a place called Hollywood Youth Hostels. I went inside.

"How much does it cost to stay here?" I asked the front desk clerk.

"Thirty-five dollars a day."

I breathed a sigh of relief. "All right," I said. I made my arrangements and put down my bags. *Wow*, I thought. *I'm here. Now what am I going to do with my life?*

But I was in Hollywood, wasn't I? List of contacts or no, I was in the very best place to make my dreams come true. I got the attention of the guy behind the reception desk again.

"Sir," I said, "where can I find Universal Studios?"

He kindly explained how I could get there and gave me the studio's phone number. I dialed. I waited. Finally, someone answered.

"My name is Ashley Shumba," I said to the voice at the other end of the line. "I've just arrived from Africa, where I'm a producer.

I am hoping for an acting job in one of your films. Do you have any jobs available?"

"Do you have an agent or manager?"

"No." I hadn't thought of that.

"There are open call auditions being held at the moment," the receptionist said. "Come tomorrow afternoon."

This is it, I thought. Perhaps I didn't know anyone in Hollywood, but I was here and already had an audition to show for it. I thought through all of my experiences in film, making a mental list of everything I had done. The exercise swelled my heart with hope that I would get one of the acting jobs I wanted so badly.

I arrived at Universal Studios the next day, excited for the audition. I assumed I would see ten or even fifteen others auditioning like me and approached the security guard with confidence, letting him know why I was there.

"See those people?" he said, pointing to a crowd of about three hundred. "Go wait with them until you're called."

Just imagine—three hundred people! All at once, I knew my chance had gotten much, much smaller. After what felt like a year, it was finally my turn to audition. I stepped in front of three people sitting at a table and introduced myself.

"We're looking for something funny," they said. "Can you be funny?"

Caught a bit off guard and feeling put on the spot, I tried to make a joke.

"Thank you."

And with those two words, I had been dismissed. I sat down again, thinking through what had just happened. Another guy approached me—I think he was a line producer.

"You have the right look for films," he offered.

"I came all the way from Africa," I said.

"Some people travel all the way from Australia," he replied, with a fair amount of kindness. "We receive millions of job applications and auditioners every year. People want to be in movies, so they travel all this way, and then they get stuck here."

Millions of people with the same dream I'd cherished my entire life? It was really something to try and wrap my head around that. But I kept listening.

"I want to give you some homework," the man said. "Go to the Hollywood Walk of Fame, where all the stars are paved into the sidewalk. Go walk around those famous areas where they have the Oscars and the Emmys and look at all the people there. Do you see great talent? Maybe some of them have it, but there are too many to put in the films we make. There are just too many."

Inside, I felt my hope, my ambition, my dream—everything—begin to crumble. I had seen what he was talking about. Not just the names bronzed in the stars or scrawled into the cement that preserved famous handprints and shoeprints in the court-yard outside Grauman's. I had also seen the street performers, the hustlers, and yes, the scores of people living on the streets. Until that moment, I'm not sure I'd recognized all those people as fellow dreamers, as people whose dreams had never become something *real*.

It shook me. And yet, the pain that came with my dismissal hit me hard. I had spent my whole life up to those moments with the kind of confidence that could only come from knowing I was *good*. I had traveled Europe. I had produced successful projects. I'd been recognized for them across my home country. Wasn't I good?

Perhaps I was. But apparently, I was also not good *enough*.

AFTER ALL, AN EXIT

I stayed in Hollywood for another week, too affected by my negative emotional spiral to do much. I couldn't eat, and I rapidly lost weight.

All the while, I thought a lot about the counsel I'd received from that line producer at Universal Studios. The full force of the truth in his words hit me in wave after wave as I observed daily life in this so-called city of dreams. How many of the people around me, living in the streets, had *really* come to Hollywood with the same kind of dream that brought me there? It seemed they also hadn't gotten the chance to be in films.

Before long, I began to wonder more about the people I saw on a daily basis. Had they continued believing that one day, they would finally see their dream come true, and had it cost them everything? Did they become homeless as a result? That was what the producer implied, and it was a harrowing thought.

Acting and film—it's a difficult industry, I realized. Life was not as rosy as it appeared in the movies and videos I had seen before coming to America. One day, I googled *how many famous people are there in the US?* A mere 28,000 out of 334 million people, the internet said. *What?* I was shocked. The realization was staggering, and I felt my hope in the arts begin to drain away.

Finally, I turned a critical eye to my own circumstances. The truth was that I was living hand to mouth, and the money I'd brought with me from Africa was rapidly dwindling. Despite having been to the United States once before, coming here had been difficult. I hadn't anticipated—or adjusted to—the skyrocketing prices of living conditions here. Inflation was high, and at that time the economic situation in America was such that even half of all Americans were living paycheck to paycheck.

I was disheartened and overcome with the very real possibility of making my bed on the streets like those I saw all around me. With each passing day, negative thoughts crept deeper into my mind. The stress ate away at my body, and I continued to lose weight. I felt a growing certainty that I was destined for poverty. Despite how hard I had worked and how much I desired a career in the arts, it felt like nothing would ever change. I began to wish desperately that I actually had money in the bank and reduced my expenses by cutting back on nonessential purchases. Still, my wish remained nothing more than that. A wish.

My goodness. I'm going to embarrass myself if I stay here, I thought. *People from home will laugh at me for coming to Hollywood. They'll say I was fired. They'll say I should have stayed in Africa. What am I going to do?*

At long last, I realized I had begun to miss my home. Compared to my experience in Hollywood, I'd had an easy life back in Namibia, complete with friends and job offers and a solid reputation upon which I could stand. But in Hollywood, I had nothing.

I should go back, I thought. I had given life a chance, but life was refusing to repay the favor. In my heart, I knew it was time to say my goodbyes—to Hollywood, to my dream of a career in the arts, and perhaps to my American dream altogether. It was time to leave.

I also needed a job—any job—that paid. And after that miserable week in Hollywood, I was ready to turn away from my pride so that I could change my life. Change began as I packed my bags and inventoried my cash. I was left with close to $300. I went back to the train station, where I'd arrived only weeks ago with so much hope and confidence. But where should I go?

I wondered if, after everything, it would be best if I *did* go back to Africa. Then again, no. Perhaps New York *was* where I needed to be. And, after all, if I could get a train ticket back to New York and things didn't work out, I could use the other half of my round-trip air ticket and go back home. This, I was forced to admit, was really the only thing that made sense. I decided on a train ticket from Hollywood to New York and checked the prices.

I didn't have enough money left. I checked on plane tickets, but they were even more expensive—about $2,000 to fly from Hollywood to New York. That certainly would not work. But I noticed that the cost of a train ticket to Philadelphia was not as expensive as one going to New York. It would take everything I had, but I could manage it.

Okay, I thought, *I've been to Philadelphia. Let me go there.*

I bought the ticket right away. As I boarded the train, I cast one last look back at Hollywood—at all the dreams that brought me there and all the things I expected to find in the city of movies and magic—and accepted reality. There was nothing waiting for me there.

CHAPTER 8
Philadelphia, City of Love

I arrived in Philly resolved to turn away from my pride and change my life through gainful employment. I didn't want to waste any time, so I stepped off the bus and went straight to a restaurant.

"I'm looking for a job," I said. "Are you hiring?"

It turned out that they were looking for a dishwasher for only three days to fill in for someone who was off on sick leave, and the manager hired me on the spot. I was thankful that I would have even *some* cash coming in, but the truth was that I felt terrible. I couldn't stop thinking of all the good I had done back in Africa. And now I was . . . washing dishes? After a few days, I'd earned a few hundred dollars, but I felt like I had lost control of my destiny. What little hope I had left drained away. Losing myself for a few hundred dollars did not seem like a worthwhile trade, so I quit the dishwashing job.

Now what? I thought.

The truth was, there were moments when I felt like my hope had completely run out. But I must've had some small amount left because I resolved to reorganize myself and find a way to move forward.

In those days, I often went to the University of Pennsylvania library to read and look for jobs online. I was there when I started to wonder what a new plan for my life might look like. I had begun to face the fact that my old plan—returning to Africa—was losing its luster. I felt that I couldn't go back because it had been announced to everyone there that I was going to America. People *expected* things of me here—big things. If I went back, they would all wonder why. They would think I had failed, and they would be right.

As the days passed, I occasionally came across opportunities for small jobs that I accepted. I washed cars, cleaned offices, and anything else that came my way to make ends meet. But the meager earnings simply weren't enough to sustain me in a major American city.

With the last money I had, I bought a bus pass. I boarded a city bus that went to the Philadelphia International Airport and was dropped off at the International Arrivals area, Terminal A, around seven o'clock in the evening.

I was heartsick. Worn out. *Hungry.* And I was staring down a grim reality.

I couldn't afford a hotel, let alone an apartment.

I couldn't afford a hot meal—or any meal, for that matter.

I certainly couldn't afford the change fee for my ticket to Africa, even if I'd wanted to go back.

My cash had run out.

I was stuck.

I looked around me at the airport lobby. Not far from where I was standing was an empty bench. I walked over and sat down, thinking I needed a moment to relax and think.

The moment wouldn't last long.

SHELTER

A few short hours later, a police officer approached me. "It's ten thirty," he said. "We're closing this section of the airport. All the international arrivals are finished for the day. I can't allow anyone to stay here. You'll have to move on."

My heart sank, but I agreed. I didn't want to upset the officer, and I understood he was only following the rules. It wasn't his fault that I was in such a precarious situation. And, after all, I'd had some time to sit and process. It hadn't been long enough, but it also wasn't nothing.

I watched as the officer went back into a small room for airport security guards and settled in behind a customer window. I longed to stay where I was, in the safety of the airport. The officer seemed reasonable enough, and I felt I could speak with him. An idea formed in my mind. It would be a longshot, but . . .

Not knowing what else to do, I gathered my courage and went to the window.

"Yes?" the officer said.

"My name is Ashley Shumba. I don't have anywhere to go, but I'm trying to figure something out," I said. "Will you allow me to stay here tonight? Only for this evening. I will leave early in the morning."

I watched his face as he studied me and considered my request. I could only imagine what he must be considering. Was I trustworthy? Would I use the opportunity to overstay my welcome?

"Passengers begin arriving very early," he began, after a few moments. "You cannot be here when they get here."

Relieved, I assured him I would be gone, thanked him for his kind generosity, then settled in for a night of sleep on one of the lounge benches. But I barely slept for all the bitter tears I cried throughout the night. I felt useless; I felt like a true failure for the first time in my life. I couldn't help but wonder what my future would look like when my present situation was growing more desperate by the hour. All night I dipped in and out of restless sleep, my mind burdened with worry as the pain of struggle carved a slow, sharp scar in my heart.

What am I going to do? I wondered. *I need a breakthrough, and I need it fast.*

Despite my fear and anguish, I found the strength to remind myself that there was light at the end of the tunnel. I might not have known what it would look like or mean for my life, but I trusted in God. The light was there because he commanded it so, and I could find confidence in that assurance.

True to my word, I rose early the next morning and left before anyone else arrived. I caught a bus and went out to search for a job again, with no plans to return to the airport. But at the end of the day, I still hadn't found anything. I was out of options and boarded a bus that would take me back to the airport. I saw the same officer from the previous day.

"I need to talk to you," I said, approaching him.

"I remember you from yesterday," he acknowledged. "Is there a problem?"

Honesty has always been my way forward, so I told him what had brought me back.

"I came from Africa to America," I said, "and I went to Hollywood for an audition. I thought I was going to have a breakthrough in film, but things didn't work out. Now I am trying to find work here. I can't go home because everyone will ask me why I spent so much money to come here if I was just going to lose everything and go back home. Many people invested money to bring me here with the hope that it would make a difference in my life. I can't let them down. I have to stay."

He listened to my outpouring, then asked questions like how

I was going to eat and where I was going to live. "You can't live here," he said, gesturing to the lounge I'd slept in the night before, "and I can only allow you to stay on the days I will be here. On the days I'm off work, they won't let you in, and I'll get in trouble if they know I let you sleep here."

I certainly didn't want him to get into trouble on my account. Still, I thought we could work something out.

"Which days are you not working?" I asked.

"Thursday and Friday."

"Okay," I said, resolving to find somewhere else to be on those days. "I won't be here on Thursday or Friday. But can we do this for two weeks?"

To my great relief, he agreed. "I can help you for two weeks. What are you going to do for a meal in the morning? I'll bring you some breakfast and a bus card that's good for a week. Because, Ashley, you need to keep going out to look for a job."

I was so moved by his generosity that I slept well that night. And in the morning, he showed up with breakfast and a bus card, just like he promised. Our plan was that I would arrive each night around ten o'clock and be gone by five-thirty the next morning. Each day, I went to eat at a shelter around 69th Street, then returned to the University of Pennsylvania library to research and apply for jobs.

By the second week, I still hadn't found anything. I arrived at the terminal one evening and found the officer waiting for me.

"Ashley," he said, "I have a problem. I've been waiting for you to come so I can explain. One of my family members is very sick, and I have to go out of state to help. I'll be gone a long time. We're going to have to find a different solution for you because I can't help you for as long as I thought."

"I understand," I said, and I really did. But I was also shaken by his news.

"There's a foundation I know of here," he continued. "They are an institution that helps provide shelter for people who need it."

"What does that mean?" I asked. "What is a shelter?"

"It's a place where people who are homeless can stay safe and get help. I want you to go there to be safe until I come back. I was talking with one of my friends and my wife, and we are thinking of ways we can help you get on your feet."

I appreciated his help. At the same time, I was taken aback by the thought of living in a place intended for people who were homeless. Was that me now? I couldn't help but think of all the people I'd seen in Hollywood, and it didn't sit well. Still, what other option did I have? I agreed to the shelter, if they would take me. He told me he would discuss it with the foundation and let me know the next morning if they could make a place for me there.

But the next morning, he sought me out right away. "Ashley, this shelter cannot take you because you aren't a US citizen," he said. "But if you say you're seeking asylum, they will let you in."

I knew what it meant to claim asylum—and I also knew that wasn't at all why I had come to America. Telling that lie might ease my present circumstances, but it would also mean I would have to live with knowing I'd been dishonest for personal gain.

"No," I said. "I can't do that. I'm not running away from anyone or anything in Africa. If I claimed asylum, it would be a lie, and I won't diminish my integrity that way."

The officer understood. I was concerned about where I would sleep the next night but felt secure in my decision to remain true to the man I wanted to be. I bedded down on my bench for what could be my last night of safe sleep, wondering where tomorrow would take me, and eventually drifted off.

Not long after, I was awakened by a group of three people. They were from public housing and asked if I would like to stay at an all-male shelter in the area. I was amazed that my circumstances could shift so suddenly. A shelter might not have been my ideal, but I no longer had to wonder where I would sleep. I thanked the group, who even helped me process my enrollment.

Slowly and slightly, my outlook was improving.

EVEN LOVE

During my time at the shelter, I witnessed what I think of as people who are *really* homeless—those who had been homeless for a long time, who understood how to navigate the systems put in place to help them, and who seemed, at least on the surface, to accept it as their way of life. I felt an immense amount of empathy for their circumstances and also knew I didn't want to remain in similar ones for any longer than was necessary. *I must find work*, I determined, *and I must find it now. If I don't, I might never be able to leave.*

One day, I decided to take a walk. While I was out, I came across a church called The Neighborhood Church. It was Sunday, I realized.

Let me go inside the church, I thought, and the idea filled me with warmth and hope. *Let me just be in a church.*

I slipped inside and looked around at the space. It felt holy and blessed—like a homecoming. A knot of tears formed in the back of my throat as I found a seat and joined the service.

After service ended, the pastor came to me. "Hello," he said. "My name is Bishop Quincy Watkins. We're having a meal today, and you are welcome to eat with us."

"Thank you," I accepted. I followed him to another room, where congregants were gathering around tables, laughing, and talking. So many of them seemed close—almost like I was looking at one large family. I took a moment to wonder where I might fit in with them, and then suddenly, I saw a beautiful young lady. I smiled at her, and she noticed it.

"Hi," she said, walking over to me. "My name is Marie. How are you?"

"I'm fine," I said, a bit stunned that she was speaking to me. "I'm Ashley Shumba. It's nice to be here with all of you."

At her invitation, I joined a group of young people for lunch, which ended with a slice of cake. Afterward, they invited me to stay longer with them, but I declined. "I was going to go to the library," I explained.

"Okay," Marie said. "Do you drive?"

"No."

"I can drop you wherever you want."

"I was also going to go to Wendy's," I said.

"Good. Let's go to Wendy's."

So we went to Wendy's. Before long, Marie was asking me about my life. I related my life story, including why I was in Philadelphia, and began to cry. "I was thinking about going back home," I said, "but I don't think I can now."

"What were you doing back in Africa? Were you a business-person? And what were you doing in Hollywood?"

"I went for an audition," I said. "And I wanted to try at being a producer like I had been back home."

"This is my first time meeting someone from Zimbabwe," she said. "Is everyone there as ambitious as you are? You have a dream, and that means a lot. You can't give up on America."

If she only knew how close I had come to doing just that. "I have no job here," I said. "No way to earn my place. I think I really have to go back."

For the moment, she seemed to accept that, and our conversation moved on to different topics. I asked what she did for a living and learned she's a registered nurse. We talked and talked—about our histories, our families, and our plans. I felt stunningly, amazingly open with her—open enough to share the types of jobs I had had to work and the humble beginnings I had come from. Was I crazy to feel that way? But Marie never judged me or looked at me with anything other than openness and respect.

Until that moment, I had not realized how much I needed someone to talk to. I hadn't known how badly I needed to vent all the years of frustration that had been bottled up inside me.

Later, when she had gone her way and I had gone mine, I found myself thinking about my life. It's often said that love is found in strange places, and maybe that's true. But love was never something I thought I would experience. Throughout my life, but especially during my stay in America, I had never given love a chance. I was busy; I was stressed. The challenges of life were far too numerous and pressing and all-consuming for me to notice one critical thing: I had isolated myself from the joy of loving and being loved.

I realized that I had always seen myself as a person with a lot of baggage, and I never wanted to drag someone else into my mess. I was a man with low confidence, afraid to love and living in fear of rejection. I centered my life around looking for opportunities to make myself better, perhaps even to make myself worthy. Once I had developed myself, I'd always thought, I could look for love.

But there I was, at one of the lowest points in my life, and I had met Marie.

The next day, Marie and I met again at the library. I like to think she realized I am a good person—ambitious and organized—and that I could be a potential partner in her life. But that second day, I told her I had decided on a plan: to go on to New York, get a job there, and eventually save enough money to return home.

"Wait," she said. "You might end up getting a job in Philadelphia."

I admired her fiery, optimistic spirit.

"I'm off work on Monday," she continued. "We can work together and send out your résumé. We'll see what we can get."

I told her that it wasn't working for me in Philadelphia, but Marie would have none of it.

"Ashley, you are in the land of hope," she said. "Just look at the journey you've traveled, and how you're still going onward. Don't give up on America—or Philly, for that matter. Just give it another try and see what life has to offer."

I agreed to do what I could to stay in America. Looking back, I always think of Marie's words as my fresh start. She made me feel like anything was possible—like I could tackle anything that was thrown at me or came my way.

Even love.

OPPORTUNITY

Marie told me she would come to check up on me each morning and afternoon or evening when she wasn't working at her job. Sometimes she brought me food. I told her that I needed to go to Western Union to collect funds that had been sent to me by my business associates in Namibia. Rosalinde and Klaudia, whom I'd worked with there, had sent me $1,000 to get by. I collected the money and deposited the entire amount into my bank account.

At the time, I was living temporarily in the shelter. I say temporarily because I was short-listed as someone in transit. Another man from Africa was there at the same time, and we became friends. He had established himself as my protector while waiting for his own citizenship papers to come in. The deputy director, Mr. Yomi Oladeinde, was from Nigeria, and he was helpful in one way and another. One day, after a visit from Marie, he pulled me aside.

"That girl," he said. "She looks like she's interested. You should ask her to lunch."

"Interested?" Despite all my realizations about love, I was still focused on finding work and moving forward. Marie was beautiful and kind, but it was unfathomable to me that she would actually be interested in me romantically. "I came here for opportunities," I said, brushing off his suggestion, "not for lunch."

"But what is a chance at love if not an opportunity?" he insisted. "Maybe you're supposed to have a life with her. And anyway, you never know why all these things are happening and why all these people are lining up to help you."

He was right about that, at least. One of those people was a lady called Tracy Leveille, who worked with the deputy director to facilitate the achievement of client wellness and autonomy through advocacy. And, thanks to the deputy director, I had been placed in a nicer area of the shelter than most who stayed there. The favoritism I'd been shown was so great it was even causing other residents to complain.

But thanks to Marie's help, within a week I had secured a job. We continued to talk, and one day, while out looking for suits I could wear to work, she said something startling.

"Ashley, I think you need to leave that shelter. I think you should move out."

"First I need to earn money so that I can pay for an apartment. I only have $1,000 in my savings, and it's not enough," I said.

"Yes, I know, but I'm working on something."

I got my clothes, and we collected my bags from where I'd dropped them for safekeeping before we went looking for suits.

"I think we need to say you're not coming back," she pressed. "Just take your bag and come with me."

"Today?"

"Right now."

I did as she asked, though I wasn't entirely sure I understood the urgency she felt. Later I would learn that she simply needed me to be independent and have my own place. I think she knew that was what I needed, too.

"Okay," she said, "for the next three days, I'm going to put you up in a hotel room while we look for different accommodations. You need to find a one-room apartment, and I will help you pay rent for the first month while you're getting your first paychecks. The second month you're earning, you can begin to help pay for yourself, and then in the third month, you can take over the payments entirely."

"Really?"

"Yes. I don't want you to be at that shelter anymore. With the little you have in your savings, combined with what I have, we can find a decent place."

PROGRESS

We followed Marie's plan, and it worked. Before long, I was living in my own apartment and supporting myself. Meeting Marie and hearing her words of encouragement and hope helped me change how I handled the many challenges mounting in my life. For the first time in a long, long while, I renewed my hope and moved forward, deciding to trust the process in spite of numerous challenges.

That is not to say anything was easy. Eventually I found work as a bus driver and part-time semitruck operator. I told myself that pride no longer mattered to me, and that what did matter was getting food on the table and being able to afford my rent. And I was able to do that, but I, like many Americans at the time, was living hand to mouth.

Despite turning from my pride, I found it difficult that I still could not afford to put money in savings or buy anything more than the barest necessities. With Marie in my life, I wanted to do more than I was able. Guilt and depressive thoughts entered my mind once again. Was I doomed to this hand-to-mouth existence? I felt like a failure.

I did not enjoy my job, but for the moment, the money meant I could remain independent and in America. For that, it was worthwhile, even if it left me feeling like the universe's punching bag. I endured hundreds of judgmental looks from people who boarded the bus each day. Disrespect and insults were regularly hurled my way, and I was expected to remain professional—in other words, to simply take it.

Society views men as strong individuals that can handle whatever is thrown at them. But I think people tend to forget that men are also human beings with emotions. For my part, I was a bus driver, watching mates my age board the bus wearing the shiny suits and taking part in the white-collar dream I'd once lived in Africa. I was educated; I had worldly and professional experience, and yet I felt barred from that dream as I drove them to and from work each day. It felt as though I was no longer directing my own dream—I was playing an extra in everyone else's.

My pride might not have mattered any longer, but my ego still prowled like a lion through me, and I took hit after hit. I felt like all the time I had spent at school was for nothing.

My experience in African culture is that depression and men's mental health are rarely talked about. Eventually I would learn that what I was experiencing during this period of my life was, in fact, depression, but I didn't have that word for it at the time. I unintentionally covered up my depression with words like "stress" and "frustration."

Meanwhile, Marie and I remained close. We enjoyed spending our Saturdays together from morning to evening, and romantic feelings were slowly blossoming between us. Marie wanted to make sure we didn't rush into a relationship, and I respected her desire to take things step by step. At the same time, I continued attending her church and making friends there. One Sunday, I spoke to the congregation about my story; I told them I had gotten a job. Afterward, one of my friends came to me.

"I have messages for you from several different people." He hesitated. "Girls."

My eyebrows went up. "Oh?"

"One wants me to tell you that she's glad you found a job and that she's happy for you. Another wants to know what you think about her and whether Marie is your girlfriend. She asked Marie to ask you if you'll go on a date with her."

I was a bit taken aback and spoke with Marie about it. She also had "messages" from her friends for me.

"If I don't give you these messages," she said, "these guys are going to be mad at me."

Suddenly I found myself at the center of interest for three people: Marie, her friend, and another girl from church. Every time we were at church together, I always talked to Marie. We were undoubtedly growing closer, but we weren't officially dating. Knowing that, the other girls at church made it a point to come talk and flirt with me, too.

The situation caught the attention of another man at church. He was an elder called Pastor Elmos Heagar, and he took me aside one Sunday. "I see what's happening, Ashley," he said. "When young girls see a guy who is single and organized like you, they tend to talk and flirt and be nice to indicate that they're ready to talk about dating, about a relationship."

I listened intently.

"I've been at this church for a while," he continued, "and I know these girls. I can tell you that Marie is not a girl—she's wife material. She's humble and good. The other ones? They may be pretty, but you'll have trouble with them."

"I will?"

He nodded. "They think they can get away with whatever they want because they're pretty. But Marie? She's realistic and has character. Go for character."

I decided he was right, and I communicated to the three that I just wanted to focus on Marie. She was the one I wanted. Marie became my girlfriend, officially, and I was elated.

WHAT WE NEED

After a while, I found an office job with a marketing company. In some ways it was better than driving the bus, but I saw right away that there was no potential for growth there. I was earning enough to keep up with my living expenses, but it was like a deadlock. I would never earn enough to move forward or change my circumstances.

No, I thought. *I cannot continue with this job.*

I couldn't deny that I was getting older. Most mates my age were either married or engaged, at the point in their lives where the struggle was largely behind them, and they were making leaps in their careers—or so I imagined. I didn't have that, but I did have Marie, and I thanked God every day for the lovely woman who became my support system and pillar of strength in tough times.

Still, I worried she would leave me for someone who had everything figured out. I worried that she was simply in a higher class than I was, and that once she realized that, she would go. But she never did. She remained by my side, giving me hope that things would be okay and revealing my purpose to live and achieve more. She had shown me that we can't do everything on our own;

sometimes we need gentle pressure to do more and wise words from others to lift us up.

Through Marie, hope kept me moving forward. I kept the life I had always pictured firmly in front of me and kept striving to earn it. I chose to believe that one day, all would be well.

In May of that year, Marie asked me about my visa. I told her it was expiring in November, and I once again was considering going back to Africa. To her credit, she took the news in stride.

"Okay, fine," she said. "But what do you think about us? We're dating, but what other plans do you have?"

"Marie, I'm not young anymore," I said. "I don't think I'll ever have the life that you want. You want a guy with ambitions. You don't want a guy like me."

"I need you to get yourself and your things together," she agreed.

Perhaps it was then that I realized I loved her.

A while later, on a better day, I resolved to take Marie out for her birthday. Before our date, I was walking through the city and passed a jewelry store. In the window, a ring sparkled in the sunlight. I thought of Marie.

And I went inside the shop.

CHAPTER 9
The Hope Remains

When I look back on that period in my life, I cannot help but feel grateful. I thank God for the lovely, smart, determined woman he placed in my life. Marie had become my support system, my strength in tough times. And times were still tough.

I had grown older. I was now past the age of being the young prodigy in the room and into the age where most people are firmly seated in their careers and either married or engaged. I was dismayed by the fact that the jobs I found myself juggling while I struggled to carve out a life in America hadn't brought me to any of those things. I worried constantly that Marie would leave me for someone who was in her class—someone who was living that white-collar dream I'd once loved as I slipped on my suit jacket each morning in Harare.

But I *was* working, and that was certainly an improvement over where I'd been when I was driven to sleep at the airport, or even when I was staying in the shelter. And, against all odds, Marie stayed. Even more than that, she infused my life with hope.

That hope fueled me. Little by little, I rediscovered a great purpose to live and achieve more. I began to believe again that the life I'd always wanted was still possible. I kept the picture of that life I wanted firmly in my mind, working tirelessly day in and day out to achieve it. I chose to believe that all would be well one day.

And why wouldn't it be, I reasoned, thinking of all the actors, musicians, and writers in America who became successful in their late thirties. *If they could do it, so can I. After all, I'm still in the land where anything is possible.*

Not many months before, all signs had pointed to the near and total collapse of Ashley Shumba. But instead of allowing the pressure to break me down, I used it as a tool to become stronger—more goal oriented and resilient. I recounted all I'd been through in Zimbabwe, and I knew one thing for certain. Now was the chance for me to rewrite my destiny. And I knew just where to begin.

WHEN THINGS ARE RIGHT

Not many days after I'd seen the ring on my walk, I took Marie out to dinner for her birthday. As we finished our meal, I said, "I have a gift for you."

"What is it?"

I passed a small box to her across the table. She opened it, and her expression changed. "Are you for real?" she asked, her voice and eyes soft.

"If you would like to get married, I would too," I said.

"I want you to know something," she said. "You're a great person. I don't see your life as it is today, I see what it will be in the future. What you've already done is remarkable, but there's something even greater in your future. I think you'll get your breakthrough someday. So yes. I will marry you."

I was elated. I still couldn't believe a woman like Marie would prefer me over all the other men in Philadelphia, but I was so very glad that she did. Her willingness to link her life with mine in marriage steeled my determination to succeed even more. After some discussion, we decided I would continue to work and save money. Then we would plan a wedding.

Happy is the man who finds a true friend, and far happier is he who finds that true friend in his wife. Such was the happiness in my life in 2013, when Marie and I married. It was a blessed moment that Marie and I still cherish to this day.

The secret of a happy marriage is finding the right person. I had found the right life partner, and marital bliss kept me positive and focused. I worked even harder to achieve more in life because I had someone to look after—and, truthfully, I also wanted to impress my bride.

After our marriage, I knew my next step was to process my immigration papers and get a green card. So one Saturday morning, Marie came to my place. She'd researched immigration lawyers in Philadelphia, and we prepared to help me take that next step. Accordingly, we made an afternoon appointment with an attorney for guidance on the process.

When we sat down in her office, she said, "Ashley's visa is still valid, and that means you don't need an attorney for his case. All you need to do is apply for permanent residence and send your filed application to the US Citizenship and Immigration Services."

Marie and I were pleased to hear that I was in such good standing, and we followed the attorney's advice exactly. Forty-five days later, I had received multiple letters from USCIS. I had also passed the required (and extensive) background checks and biometric and medical appointments to verify my identity and clear me of communicable diseases.

Now there was only one appointment left: an interview to determine if my marriage to Marie was legitimate. We arrived at our interview appointment early in the morning and were almost immediately shown to separate interview rooms. We were both asked questions about our relationship, as well as each other's personality and family backgrounds. After a half hour, the woman who had taken us to separate rooms returned. She escorted Marie and I back to her desk.

"Congratulations," she said. "Everything is genuine. I should also say that Ashley's immigration record is impeccable. I'm very impressed. In fact, out of all the applications I've processed, this one is record-breaking. Welcome to America!"

Practically speaking, it took me less than four months to be approved as a permanent resident of the United States. After that, I knew Marie and I would eventually become parents. We had a long road to travel together before then, but I looked forward to the day we would share the blessing of children.

MAKING UP FOR LOST TIME

Despite my refusal to return to school in the early days of my producing career in Zimbabwe, I held another long-cherished dream: to study and advance my qualifications in the USA. America is regarded as one of the top places in the world for scientific and creative endeavors and is known across the globe for its brilliant students and their achievements. Stories of the people who studied in the US have always been inspirational to me.

So it was with great pleasure that I learned of my acceptance to Widener University Delaware Law School in 2015. I was grateful that student loans and timetables created to accommodate a working schedule allowed me the flexibility to realize the dream of a college degree. I would be able to attend school while continuing to work my full-time job and two part-time jobs.

My experience of higher education in America was an eye-opening one. I saw firsthand the eclectic mix of people from so many different countries; I heard them speak of a myriad of cultural beliefs and ethical values. Learning how to navigate this wonderful mix improved my people skills to the degree that I began to feel comfortable interacting with individuals of differing origins and have fun while doing it. I met amazing people pursuing the same degree program as I was. I am now happy to call them friends.

Still, my educational path was not necessarily an easy or simple one. University studies are demanding on their own, but I was also managing an overstuffed work schedule and my responsibilities at home. But I was determined to get good grades and become one of the most respected students at the school, just as I had all those years ago when I was away at boarding school as a youth.

My parents always instilled in me and my siblings that we should do whatever we could to bring a smile to another. Thus I endeavored to help other students who were failing to understand our lectures gain a better understanding of the course materials and succeed. Although my own goals were often pushed aside so that I could help others achieve theirs, I was honored to be a help. It is always close to my heart.

Alongside my law studies, I also took extra classes to meet the requirements for international students, eventually passing the state program with concentrations in English, American history, advanced mathematics, and world geography. With my regular degree program and my three jobs, I worked eighteen-hour days.

Keeping up with that schedule meant being hard on myself and making sacrifices. I personally deprived myself of many things I would have liked to do or have during that period of my life, but I believed the sacrifices were worth it in the long run. In my case, staying focused and continuing to work toward my goals resulted in growing distance between myself and the friends who thought I was aiming for the impossible. To them, my dream was only that—a dream. However, *I* knew I was on the right path. I was still moving through the process of achievement, but I knew exactly where I was heading. With my supportive wife beside me, I refused to back down or give up on that dream for any reason.

Now, I can indeed say that it's possible to achieve so many things in this life, so long as you remain focused and committed. Certainly, it was challenging, but everything I did was to make up for the time I felt I lost and to carve out a better life for myself and my family.

LEGACY MAN

One day, while Marie and I were making our way home from church, I convinced her that we should go and look at houses. We drove through several areas, one of which was a luxury community.

"Look," I pointed out, surveying the empty lots, "there are available stands here."

"There are," she said, "but I don't think our finances will qualify us for that kind of loan yet."

"We'll see," I said, having already made up my mind to inquire.

I felt the bright bloom of hope in my heart. In the time it took to get to the site office, I became convinced that one of those empty stands was going to be our home address. We spoke to the site manager, and I shared my story with her, inquiring about the empty stands.

"I'm touched by your story," she said, "and how you came to this country and have worked so hard to achieve more. We need more people like you in America. If there is anything I can do to make your life and your journey easier here, I will do my best to help."

She politely asked if I had the funds to put down a deposit that day. If so, she informed me, we could begin the process of qualifying for the mortgage loan we would need to fund the lot purchase and the construction of our new home.

I looked at Marie. I knew she wasn't completely comfortable with committing to such a large loan, but I could also see the hope shining in her eyes. It matched the certainty in my heart—certainty that God would make a way for us. She and I were two people combined with the same mindset and a single goal. Together, and with God leading the way, we could do this. A cord of three strands is not easily broken.

"Yes, I have the funds," I said to the manager, "and I am happy to write the check today."

And just like that, I withdrew my checkbook, wrote a check for our future home, and accepted a stack of papers to begin signing. With each flourish of my pen, my heart sang, "I am a homeowner, I am a homeowner, I am a homeowner . . ."

Never in my wildest dreams had I imagined that I—a man of humble beginnings, who experienced homelessness, drove a bus for a living, and nearly went back to Africa when life in America felt like too much to bear—would one day own land in a country where almost everyone I knew back home dreams of beginning a new life. It was an extraordinary moment.

Marie and I left the site feeling incredibly happy. We met with a mortgage officer shortly afterwards and were approved for the loan we needed. Before long, construction on our future home began, and we became the youngest couple in the community when we moved into our house in October 2015. By many standards, including mine, it was a mansion—far bigger than Marie and I needed.

But walking through the rooms of our new home, I couldn't help but picture my own humble beginnings. Instead of smooth walls and vaulted ceilings, I saw thatched houses. Instead of a gleaming kitchen with modern appliances and running water, I saw myself using firewood for cooking and making the long-distance trek each day to fetch water to the house. Instead of bedroom after bedroom after bedroom, there I was—sharing rooms with three or four cousins and siblings, without any privacy at all. I even remember sleeping in the dining room at times to accommodate everyone in our house.

I took a deep breath. Such was my history. And while it was good in its own ways, it also disadvantaged me in many others. I didn't want that for my future children. Looking around me, I was warmed by the fact that I wanted more for them and had refused to settle for anything less. Whenever my children chose to appear, they would enter a home that, in so many ways, represented the legacy I'd spent my whole life building. Leaving that legacy had always been such a large part of my dream. I wanted desperately to make a name for myself that was recognized across the globe—this was, in some ways, why my Hollywood dreams had been so attractive and why, when they proved fruitless, they had cut me to the bone.

But in the years since, I'd learned well that the American Dream can play out in a variety of ways. The United States offers bountiful opportunities to citizens, immigrants, and nonresidents alike. Owning a business in America, I learned, was possible for many. And as long as my papers and documentation were in order, business ownership was possible for *me*.

Armed with this knowledge—and with thankfulness in my heart for the prescience that kept me from ever violating my immigration status—I knew I must act on my dreams of entrepreneurship. Building a business would be one more part of the legacy I would leave my future children. So the same year Marie and I moved into our house, I registered and founded my own trucking company.

As always, the old fears of failing were present in my mind. But I have learned that while the most successful entrepreneurs are optimistic, they are often simultaneously frustrated, anxious, and afraid. Being in the business world has taught me that these are all normal emotions to have while moving forward, and that the real challenge only comes when you give into them. To paraphrase Oprah Winfrey, challenges are gifts that force us to search for a new center of gravity. Instead of fighting them, we simply must find a new way to stand.

I have always found that the harder I work, the more luck I seem to have. But my secret has always been to take the risks that will allow me to grow. I always take calculated risks. Things don't always go smoothly—they're not supposed to—but what you do in the rough patches is what matters. And, if at first you don't succeed, as they told us in primary school, *try, try, try again.*

With those thoughts guiding me, I acknowledged my old fears of failure but learned to stand on the things I had accomplished and built since coming to this country. Recounting my successes, setting goals, and allowing myself to start small helped me keep a positive mindset and move forward—always with my children in mind.

Marie and I both had steady incomes; we had our beautiful new home. All that remained was to fill it with children. Soon Marie was pregnant with twins, and we eagerly anticipated the arrival of our children. But tragedy struck us when, in 2017, both our babies died before birth. I can only say that it was one of the worst things I have ever experienced.

We had decorated two rooms of our home, and now we had to repaint and throw away all the clothes and furniture we had purchased for our lovely girls. Every morning, Marie would scream, "My babies! Why, Lord? Why?" It took six months to process the loss, and we weren't the only ones attempting to do so. My parents and Marie's parents also experienced severe grief. My dad had visited us before and was looking forward to welcoming his first twin grandchildren. The pain we felt is still unbearable to this day. It is still so sharp and feels like being torn apart. Every August, we commemorate the twins with prayers and fasting. It has been the only way we can find slow healing and peace.

I think many will understand when I describe the loss as traumatic, for myself and for my wife. For me, seeing Marie endure such pain and cry so many tears was a trauma second only to losing our twins. Had I not had a lifetime of recovering from hardship before that moment, I could easily have been lost to it too. Instead, I was able to cling to the hope that one day, we would hold our healthy children in our arms, and that the legacy I continued to build would go to them.

KINDLING

It is apparent to anyone who knows me that creation is simply part of who I am. After the losses I've experienced, I now have no fear in starting projects.

The year after Marie and I lost our twins, I embarked on another creative project: founding the Global Small Business Awards program to appreciate small business entrepreneurs who were, and still are, making positive change in the world. My hope was to motivate others to follow their lead, regardless of the size of their business.

I have always understood how much appreciation can help someone attain their goals. For instance, my family was always appreciative of my efforts, and their enthusiasm helped me immensely as I moved forward. I also know from experience just how motivating appreciation can be when it comes from someone who is also anchored in the business world. Other businesspeople are my compatriots—those who have experienced similar struggles as I did while starting something new.

As I built the Global Small Business Awards program, my attempts at recognition found their own recognition. Another group of entrepreneurs who heard of my program and, like other interested parties who wanted to invest in the program, desired to help move it forward contacted me and invited me to meet with them in Dubai. Once again, I found myself boarding an international flight with the beginnings of a production glimmering on the horizon. It was a small spark—but a spark, nonetheless.

My visit to Dubai lasted three days, culminating with a plan to stage the awards in 2020. On my flight home, I couldn't ignore the way that small spark had kindled the tinder of an old dream in my heart.

As Leviticus says, there are seasons for everything, and when I returned home, I learned that a season in Marie's and my life that had passed was being renewed. God, in his infinite grace, had allowed her to become pregnant again.

A CRASH LANDING

One November day, when Marie's pregnancy had reached its ninth month, I picked her up for some shopping. Her due date was rapidly approaching; it was a Sunday, and our baby was due the following Wednesday. Marie climbed into our Jeep Grand Cherokee looking radiant. She fastened her seatbelt, and I pulled onto the street, heading for the supermarket to purchase what we needed in preparation of our baby's arrival.

Despite the gray November skies overhead, having my wife beside me made the day lovely, and I was enjoying the ride. Then suddenly, WHAM! We were jolted by an intense, metal-crushing impact on Marie's side of the Jeep as another car barreled into us at full speed. I blinked rapidly to clear my vision and understand what had happened. Beside me, Marie began to panic.

"The baby, the baby," she said, protectively holding her swollen belly.

I found my phone—it was, thankfully, operational—and called an ambulance. I didn't want to alarm Marie more, but I was scared too. I couldn't help but think of her last pregnancy; I couldn't help but remember so much hope shattered by such staggering loss. I prayed that this would end differently.

At the hospital, we learned that Marie's blood pressure had skyrocketed because of the crash and ensuing panic. Our baby's heartbeat was uneven and continued to go up and down, up and down, up and down.

"I'm afraid your baby might have been affected during the impact," Marie's doctor said, taking care to speak calmly and with gentle assurance. "We need to induce your labor now."

Marie was quickly admitted to labor and delivery. The nurses and doctors carried out their tasks admirably, but in the end, Marie was taken to the operating room for an emergency cesarean section. I was called into the OR with my wife and witnessed the entire process.

Through it all, God heard my prayers for the health of my loving wife and precious child. Marie safely delivered a healthy baby boy that day. In my overwhelming relief and happiness, I named him

Asher. Since his eventful arrival into this world, Asher has filled our once empty house with blessings and joy.

STILL STRIVING

By that point in my life, I was living the American Dream. I had a beautiful family, I owned my own home, and I even had a salaried job with benefits and a 401K. I was light years away from the Ashley Shumba who had needed to partake of a stranger's kindness just to spend his nights sleeping on a bench in an airport lounge. In so many ways, I had achieved the picture I'd held in my mind for so long. Through hard work, long days and nights, and the true partnership with my wife, my dream had become a reality. *Almost.*

"Marie," I said one day, "I want to join the limousine business."

"What?"

"The people we want to meet in this world use limousines," I explained. "Celebrities, businesspeople, those with the wealth and means to make a difference. Deep in my heart, I believe this is the next step in my path."

"Okay..."

She might not have been fully convinced yet, but I felt the conviction in my bones. I was at another crossroads—one that necessitated I take another calculated risk.

"Give me one year," I said.

And to her everlasting credit, she did.

CHAPTER 10

American Dreams Do Come True

For a good long while before Marie and I had that conversation, I'd decided I would just work and raise my family; that was it. But then, despite having to give up a good salary with benefits, I leapt into the limousine industry.

Marie and so many others continued to wonder how I could leave such a stable, secure job as the one I had. Even my best friend in Africa wrote to me and said, "Ash, don't do it."

But despite—or perhaps because of—how many times I've fallen down in life, I don't doubt my abilities or potential. I am a man of confidence.

Like so many other leaps in my life, entering the limousine industry was a calculated risk. I started becoming active in 2021, during the COVID-19 pandemic. I determined that if it didn't pan out in that year, I would forget it, just like I'd promised Marie. And I would have.

But then, in 2022, I met Brian Dawkins. To this day I cannot believe what happened next.

WELCOME TO AMERICA

My stay in the US has been graced with so many impactful encounters. One snowy day in 2022, dispatch informed me that my next passenger's flight had experienced a weather-related change of course. Instead of arriving at Atlantica Aviation Airport in Philadelphia, his flight had been diverted to Delaware, and I was to pick him up there.

It was snowing like crazy, and the drive took longer than usual. I knew I would make it on time, but just barely. Upon my arrival at the airport, I went straight to the arrival desk to inquire about my passenger's flight. I was informed that Mr. Irsay's plane would be landing in five minutes, and I was to drive toward the main arrival gate. I did as instructed, and after a few minutes, I saw a large plane emblazoned with the word "COLTS" in blue and white.

Yes, my Mr. Irsay was, in fact, *the* Jim Irsay, owner of the Indianapolis Colts football team, and a billionaire. One look at that plane, and I knew he had arrived. I parked my limo adjacent to Mr. Irsay's plane and got out. The weather was chilly and peppered with snow showers, but I wanted my passenger to know that I was waiting for him and ready to assist in any way I might be needed. Another van, designated to carry extra luggage and some members of his team, pulled up behind me.

Before long, the plane's cabin door opened, and its stairs lowered to the ground. I sprang into action and climbed the stairs to begin collecting luggage.

On a different day, I might have had help. But the conditions outside had rapidly devolved from bad to brutal, and no one came outside other than Mr. Irsay's bodyguard and personal assistant—not even the driver of the van that had pulled onto the tarmac behind me.

After I had loaded about five bags, I saw an individual with an unmistakable air of wealth and personality about him being helped down the plane steps. I went to the passenger door and stood ready to open it for him.

"Thank you for coming to pick us up," Mr. Irsay said upon coming face-to-face with me.

"My pleasure, sir. It's nice meeting you." I held the door so that he, along with his daughter, bodyguard, and assistant, could escape the cold, then closed it tightly against the wintery conditions swirling all around. With the car loaded and my passengers ensconced in warmth, I climbed into the driver's seat and prepared to pull away from the plane. I started to close the partition and give my passengers some privacy.

"Don't close it," they said cheerfully. Then, to my great surprise, Mr. Irsay reached through the opening and touched my shoulder.

"What's your name and where are you from?" he asked.

As I answered, I looked up and saw him smiling in the rearview mirror. "I was watching you from the plane window. You were the only one willing to help in this awful weather. Thank you for that."

With those words, Mr. Irsay handed me a strap of crisp $100 bills (totaling $2,000)—to me, a shocking amount, and certainly the largest tip I'd ever received. I was speechless at his generosity and genuine warmth.

"Welcome to America," he said.

HOW TO CHANGE A LIFE

Generous tips aside, driving Jim Irsay was a wonderful experience. Our drive was filled with quiz games and discussions that I was encouraged to join. We even exchanged our contact details. Sometimes it happens that way—I meet a stranger once and enjoy a single, pleasant experience.

Other times, my driving assignments evolve into lifelong friendships full of mutual support. Such was the case one morning, when I received a call from a travel agent. They asked if I could access a car that would accommodate driving ten people to an upcoming Phillies game. I said I thought I could, and after hanging up the phone I reached out to one of my contacts and managed to reserve a limo bus.

Instead of hiring a driver for this particular job, I decided to take the assignment myself. I drove to the pickup address and found myself in front of a large, comfortable looking home. A man I could only assume was my passenger came through the front door to meet me.

"Hello," I said, getting out of the car to shake the man's hand. "I'm Ashley Shumba, your driver for today."

"I'm John Glomb," he said. "Thank you for coming."

We chatted for a moment, and he asked about my accent. I told him the short version of my story and that I had immigrated from Africa.

"Would you like to come inside?" he asked. "You're quite welcome here."

I followed him in. To my surprise, John immediately introduced me to his beautiful wife and lovely children. "Everyone, please meet and greet Ashley Shumba. He's an international man from Zimbabwe."

To my even bigger surprise, John's family all began to hug me as if we had known each other all our lives.

"Ashley, please help yourself to anything you like in the refrigerator," John said. "We keep a lot of global items in our fridge, and you're welcome to it all."

This man is a very generous and good person, I thought as I helped myself to a bottle of Coca-Cola and a bottle of water. I was amazed at how welcomed I felt in a stranger's home. And I hadn't even experienced half of it. As we were about to leave the house, John asked if I would take a photo with his family. I agreed and spent a few enjoyable minutes taking selfies with his kids. Afterward, everyone piled into the limo bus. Our trip to the stadium was filled with laughter and lively discussions on topics ranging from culture to family to opportunities to celebrities. It was one of the most unique and interesting drives I've ever been on, before or since.

Upon our arrival at the stadium, John asked if I would like to join his family for the game. I would have liked to have accepted his generous offer, but I felt my responsibilities to my job came first. I declined so that I could keep an eye on the limo bus. But I was moved by his warmth and generosity. I went home to my family, glad for the intuition that had pushed me to take that particular job.

The next day, while I was at home, I received a call from a woman named Anita Smith. She identified herself as John Glomb's executive assistant and said he had asked her to pass a message along to me.

"John asked me to tell you that he was completely impressed with your services yesterday," Anita said. "From now on, he would like you to be responsible for shuttling his family and members of his office."

As it turned out, his office was none other than Philadelphia Insurance Companies—one of the largest insurance companies in the US and the world, where he served as president and CEO. Even without the knowledge that he helmed a multi-billion-dollar company, I would have been thrilled to receive such a call and its offer of steady business.

"Thank you," I said, the happiness evident in my voice. "I am grateful for Mr. Glomb's generosity and would love to make myself available to him whenever I am needed."

About a month later, Anita called to ask if I could be available to pick up one of John's business associates, Ian Brimecome. Ian, she told me, is the chairman of Tokio Marine—a sister company to Philadelphia Insurance—and his international flight would land later that day in New York. I accepted and drove the two hours to John F. Kennedy International Airport in Queens, New York.

Right away, I was impressed with Ian and could see why he and John got along so well. Ian was incredibly friendly. All the way back to Philadelphia, we talked about soccer, business, families, and Africa. Ian shared that he was in charge of three companies with combined assets in the tens of billions. I was already impressed with his affability, but when I learned where he stood in the business world, I was shocked at how someone on the Fortune 500 top executive list could be so humble and down to earth. I was glad to feel like I was in good books with someone as well-regarded as he.

I thought of Ian, John, and Brian—three people I wouldn't have met if I hadn't taken the calculated risk of entering the limousine industry. *My goodness. These are people everyone in the world is trying to meet.*

When I dropped Ian at his hotel, he thanked me for the safe driving and conversations about business. He let me know that he planned to tell John what a great experience it was too. To me, the whole day seemed fortuitous in the same way it had been when I encountered Bilaal Ameen on the streets of Harare, met the American diplomat, and walked into a random church one Sunday morning and met the woman who would one day become my wife.

What kinds of opportunities could grow from the seeds of goodwill that had been planted by John, Ian, and I? I wondered. Only time would tell.

TO GOD BE THE GLORY

Not long after getting to know John and Ian, I received the fateful job assignment that brought Brian Dawkins into my story. That afternoon, as we sat discussing my life in the car in front of his hotel, he asked if I would call my wife so that he could meet her on video chat. I rang her and she immediately answered.

"Marie," I said, before passing the phone to Brian, "someone wants to say hello."

"Oh my goodness!" she exclaimed as Brian turned the camera on himself. "Are you Brian Dawkins?"

"Yes, I am," he confirmed warmly. "I just wanted to tell you that I have had a very fruitful conversation with your husband. Ashley has such a unique and inspiring story, and I would like to see it scripted into a book and then a movie."

As they chatted, I sat back against the seat, stunned. His mention of a film about my life—could it be possible? I felt as if I had closed the door on my Hollywood dreams so many years before. But could it be that God, in his infinite wisdom and with his perfect timing, had chosen to open it again? I had not been able to make this particular dream come true on my own, though I had tried so hard, so many times. But one thing I knew for certain was that if God willed it, he would make it happen.

As I witnessed his providence and favor in my life once again—and in a way that was so deeply personal to me and spoke to such a long-cherished dream of my heart—I felt a lifetime's worth of gratitude and hope lift my spirit.

"Please keep up the good work you both are doing," Brian continued, still speaking to Marie, "both for your family and for the country."

After they ended the call, Brian was also kind enough to speak with one of my friends, Edward Gall, who is an Eagles fan.

Edward said to me, "Ashley, that man you are sitting next to is well-respected in American football. That's a great football player you're taking to his destination and a man of God. You don't get a lot of people like Brian Dawkins; enjoy the conversation."

Yes, I thought, *I certainly am. Not only in Brian's, but also in God's.*

After the flurry of conversation had passed, Brian asked if he could pray with me. I readily agreed, and he asked God to give us strength in the days ahead as we moved forward with the book project. I hadn't known before that moment that Brian was a man of such unshakeable faith, but the understanding was impressed powerfully upon me then. I felt humbled and elated. This great man, like so many others in my story, had truly been sent by God.

IN AN INSTANT

One morning I received a call from John Glomb's assistant Anita. She asked if I could pick up John and his wife the following morning at five o'clock and drive them to the airport.

"Of course," I answered.

I arrived on time the next morning to collect my passengers, and John's wife opened the kitchen door to ask if I needed anything. I thanked her, but said no. It was just too early for me to have anything to eat or drink. I loaded their bags, and we set off for Philadelphia International Airport. On this particular drive, my phone was connected to the car's audio through Bluetooth. Unbeknownst to me, my notifications were set to full volume.

"YOU HAVE A TEXT MESSAGE FROM BRIAN DAWKINS," the car speakers shouted through the car.

"Is that Brian Dawkins, the former Eagles player?" John asked, surprise written all over his face.

"It is," I said. I glanced at the text message. "He's wishing me a happy Father's Day."

"It's wonderful that you know him well enough to text with him," John continued. "How did you two meet?"

"The same way I met you," I said, with a fond smile, "but with a few more bumps in the road."

I related the story. "And after all that," I concluded, "Mr. Dawkins is putting together a team to write a book about my life experiences." I felt like a superstar on a live television reality show. Having the unique opportunity to share my life story and see others be inspired by it was, and still is, remarkable. (Even to this day I can hardly believe the entire project and book are about my life story. It's amazing and very humbling, but with God all things are possible.)

"Really?" One glance at my friend in the rearview mirror told me I'd piqued his interest.

By the time I filled in all the details and answered all their questions, we had arrived at the airport. Once again, I helped with their bags and wished them both a safe flight. I turned back to the car.

"Ashley," John said, "I knew something more was happening in your life, and now my suspicions are confirmed. I would like to hear more about your book project when I get back. If you need any assistance to make it happen, please feel free to contact Anita and schedule a meeting with me."

What a unique opportunity! I was incredibly happy. "I will keep you posted," I promised. We parted ways, and I considered how wonderful it was to know such kind, generous people.

I took John at his word and called Anita, who scheduled the meeting. I arrived at the Philadelphia Insurance Companies office about fifteen minutes before two o'clock on the appointed afternoon to get situated and familiarize myself with the environment.

I marveled at the space—an enormous, magnificent building of glass. I began to sweat.

Before long, Anita appeared to escort me to the executive offices. When we stepped into the suite, I could see everyone whispering. They were attempting to hide their words, but the covert glances they darted my way conveyed everything. "Who is this guy, and why is he being shown such respect?"

Now I was *really* getting nervous. I sat down in a handsome leather chair—one of many in the massive office—and tried to collect myself. I couldn't say why, but I had a sense that my moment had arrived. I was impressed by a sudden, heavy certainty that everything in my life before—every struggle, dream, heartache, failure, and inch of progress—had led me here. I was staggered by the weight of that intuition. If this was indeed my opportunity for breakthrough, what would happen if the meeting went poorly?

The minutes ticked by. *God will make a way*, I reminded myself.

Suddenly, John popped his head around a corner. "Hi Ashley," he said. "Welcome to our offices. I'm excited about this book project and want to hear more about it. I hope it's all right, but I told Ian about this opportunity ahead of your arrival. If there's anything we can do to help you achieve your goals, feel free to ask."

I took a breath. "Would you ask your friends in the corporate world to attend my book launch and perhaps partner with me in the project in some small way or another?" I asked.

"How far along have you gotten in the project?" he asked.

I summarized what we had accomplished and what we still needed in the way of writing, editing, printing, publishing, and launching my book. And I waited.

"Ashley," John said, "you are a truly exemplary person—honest, reliable, and always kind to my family and staff. You have worked so hard. As a token of appreciation, I would like to do all that you have just asked and more."

At his words I simply froze. Tears of joy formed in my eyes, then spilled down my cheeks and around my chin. I had come prepared to ask for introductions, and yet my friend—I knew he had become that—was willing to do so much more. At that moment, I realized God had truly answered my prayers. He had already given me so much of my American dream, and now he was truly going to give me the rest of it.

John was unfailingly true to his word and has been an incredible source of support ever since. After our meeting that day, I immediately called Brian and shared this new, wonderful development.

"Even though I wanted to give you the kind of help he's promised," Brian said, "I knew you would somehow find a way."

Everything moved quickly after that. More meetings and Zoom calls were arranged; our team, including John, Brian, authors Justin Batt and Alex Demczack, Chloie Benton, and Mandi Reed from Streamline Books began working on the project. Everyone was pleased to come together in a unified spirit to bring this book—this record of my history—to life.

For my part, it's still difficult to believe that I am now Ashley Shumba, *author*, and that I may still one day be Ashley Shumba, *film producer*. But then I look back across the years, across my experience as an immigrant in multiple countries, and remember.

I thought my life was full of shame, but to some it was full of strength.

Throughout my life, those people have consistently praised how diligently I strove to be a person of character. I never violated my immigration status in any country. I have never been violent or committed a crime or been arrested—or even received a warning. That's not to pat myself on the back or put myself up on a pedestal, but only to say to other youths that *you can also rise*. Value your honest character above all else, work—really *work*—to preserve it, follow the rule of law, and watch what God will do with your faithfulness.

I'm just an ordinary citizen, an ordinary person who feels humbled to know that there are people in this world who really have love in their hearts. There are people who are thoughtful and people who really feel like others should be given the opportunity to be successful—and who go out of their way to help. And sometimes, inexplicably, those people travel from Europe by private plane to attend your book launch.

Can you imagine?

In this country, they call a story like mine "living the American Dream." I certainly thought of it that way. But now I know a few things about that American Dream, and I can promise you something.

You can make that dream your American *reality*.

CONCLUSION
What You Do with What You Have

When I came to America, things started out for me on a very bad note. But I soon learned that this is a country where people have so much love in their hearts.

I also learned that it is truly a country where people believe in their dreams and encourage each other to do the same. This is a country where, if you have a good character, are hardworking and focused, your dreams can come true. This country has given me means, love, and a family. Simply put, it has given me life. For that, it will be eternally close to my heart.

But I have always seen myself as a citizen of the world.

Like those wonderful people in America who have given of themselves and their resources to help me succeed, I have always been focused on helping others in whatever small way I can. From the time I was in Namibia and volunteered to pay the school fees for children who would otherwise not have the opportunity to gain an education, I have tried to give back.

My efforts accelerated during the COVID-19 pandemic, when I made it my mission to provide food for the villagers in my home country of Zimbabwe. The pandemic hit hard everywhere, but in Africa the lockdowns and closures severely impacted rural communities. Multifaceted economic and social consequences of the pandemic exposed structural inequalities. In too many cases, these communities had no one to help or stand up for them. As a result, many people in Africa died—most because they were forced to leave their homes just to acquire food for their families and contracted the virus in the process.

Those widespread deaths created additional horrors: children in secondary school who have been forced to drop out to care for their younger siblings; a sharp rise in early childhood marriages; and an increase in the prostitution of young children, who enter the trade in the hope of earning money to provide food for their siblings. As you can imagine, there has been a corresponding increase in adolescents who have become HIV positive.

Between 2021 and 2022, once the World Health Organization lifted travel bans, I traveled extensively back to Zimbabwe to help my community during these difficult times. God had blessed me enough to do so and had protected my family in America, and I felt the tug on my heart to help protect my family in Africa. I started a food bank that also cooked and served hot meals to impacted members of the community. Every day, thirty bellies that would otherwise have been empty were filled. We also partnered with the local clinic and other nongovernmental organizations to provide medical aid.

It never seemed like enough, but it made a difference to the families we were able to reach. And, at the end of each day, when I saw the smiles that graced children's faces after a meal, I was moved. I always wanted to do more.

Aid was necessary and helpful in those days, but I wanted to give them a net, so to speak, and teach them to fish for themselves. My larger goal was to help my community and people rebuild after experiencing such immeasurable loss during the pandemic. Businesses had been destroyed, companies had closed, and much of the adult workforce was simply gone. People grieved so many things in so many ways. But I knew I could apply what I had learned in America and equip my fellow mates to improve their lives. Thus I began a farming project in Zimbabwe that included several varieties of crops and even livestock. Ultimately, more than twenty people were permanently employed to care for the farm, and gradually the economic and social living standards improved. Small farms began springing up all around, and the sense of unity in my community grew.

Now, each time I return to my village, the entire village turns out to see me. I think, in part, they want to be able to say, "This person who has given so much truly does exist." I understand that because sometimes I still pinch myself when I think of what Brian Dawkins, John Glomb, and Ian McVey have done for me. But I also often get requests from families who are still struggling despite all the improvements. They ask if I can help pay for their children to go to school. But in my heart, I know they need that and so much more.

That is why, with this book, I plan to channel all proceeds to the Ashley Shumba Foundation to help less privileged children. I am so very grateful to feel the support of my American friends, businesses, and organizations coming around me. Since I have been so blessed to be connected with so many doctors and people in business, I plan to build children's homes in Africa, and eventually, a children's hospital. My hope is to begin in my village and then keep building outward.

See, I may be Ashley Shumba, author, but I am also a child of my village. I was born in that village, raised in that village, and educated there for the first part of my life. In so many ways, my life is in that village. Yes, America is my home and my country, and I love it dearly. But I will not forget that my feet are rooted in African soil.

I always tell people that Africa is a young continent. That's because in Africa, the majority of people are young people. I feel an urgency to make it possible for them to access the things they need—things like food, clean water, shelter, and healthcare. Without providing those things, we are destroying the very foundation of Africa's future.

As much as I love this book, I must confess that for me, it isn't about the book. Perhaps I once craved fame and recognition, but I am no longer that person. I simply want to be remembered as someone who did everything he could to change people's lives for the better. My education and experience may be small in the grand scheme of things, but I can use them to make a positive impact in the lives of others.

Won't you join me?

ACKNOWLEDGMENTS

First, I would like to acknowledge my mum and dad, siblings, uncles, aunties, cousins, in-laws, and friends who played a major role in my upbringing. Second, my everlasting love goes to the family I have created—my wife (Marie) and my three children (Asher, Alexander, and Alysha). Third, my special respect and appreciation goes to my brother Brian Dawkins, for initiating the book project. It was such a life-changing suggestion. Thank you and may God bless you! Finally, my special appreciation goes to the following individuals and organizations for making this publication possible:

- Anania and Faith Shumba (Mum & Dad)
- Thulani and Thelma Shumba (siblings)
- Biriam and Audrey Wabatagore
- Marie Blandine Paul-Shumba
- Brian Dawkins Sr. (NFL Hall of Fame)
- John W. Glomb Jr.
- Philadelphia Insurance Companies
- Streamline Books
- Ashley Shumba Foundation

- Global Small Business Awards
- Bilaal Ameen
- Justin Batt
- Chloie Benton
- Mandi Reed
- Abigael Elliott
- Ian McVey
- Margaret Richards
- Edward and Leslie Gall
- Rosalinde Nakale
- Kiki Divaris
- Nyarai Wenjere
- Stephen Mushonga
- Mungushi Dion
- Dawn Parkinson
- David Peech

www.ingramcontent.com/pod-product-compliance
Lightning Source LLC
Chambersburg PA
CBHW061759120626
46550CB00005B/2056